CAP'N
DELL'S

s t o r i e s

---

by William Odell Spain 4-30-05

William Odell Spain

To: Mrs. Reba Meekless
a fine family and
long history Name of the
Aried

CHAPEL HILL
PRESS, INC.

Earlier versions of many of these stories were originally published
in the *Pamlico News.*

ISBN Number 1-880849-45-3
Library of Congress Catalog 2002106198

Manufactured in the United States of America
08 07 06 05 04   10 9 8 7 6 5 4 3 2

To the people of Goose Creek Island and our way of life

Cap'n Dell's Stories

Introduction

In 1955, when I got my first shrimp boat, the only luxury we had was a two-channel radio. There were a lot of boats, and most of the time the captain who had the strongest radio did the most talking. Mine wasn't too strong, but I managed to do my part of talking, along with my friends. We held our own in that area!

One of my friends was Clyde Smith of Mesic. We worked together at the fish house for a number of years, and everybody called me Odell. One year, Clyde was out on a boat he was working for someone else, and it had the luxury of having a radio. I heard him talking over the radio to other captains, so I called him. Clyde stuttered when he talked, but not too bad. He stuttered a lot like Mel Tillis. Everybody knew it, and just waited for him to get his words out.

One day, we were all working in the Sound. It was a beautiful day with calm seas, and most of the captains who had the stronger radios had lain down. Some people used to say when the radios got quiet "what a blessing it was." They said the same thing about us, so the channels were pretty well clear.

We were barely catching enough to work on, so there wasn't much taking place on deck. But there was a lot of talking going on over the radios to pass the time. Clyde called me, using just the name of my boat, and I answered him. He could say "Odell" or "Cap'n" with no problem, but when he tried to put them together (Captain Odell), it took him a while to get it all out. I could hear him working on it and it sounded like Capt-u-dell or r-dell, ah-dell, or capt-by-jon—dell, when he finally got it out. The "O" messed it up for him.

That particular day, we talked a lot about important things and Clyde was about worn out trying to get my name out. This went on for a week, before he began to shorting it up and just saying "Cap'n."

Finally he got to saying "Cap'n Dell", and he had no problem with that. From then on, he would just call me Cap'n Dell. The other men working the boats also started calling me Cap'n Dell. It spread like wildfire, and that name is still with me today.

When I go to the fish house, I'm Cap'n Dell. If I go around any of the workboats, they call me Cap'n Dell. My children called me "Daddy" or "Father" when they were little, but when they got bigger, I was Cap'n Dell to them, too.

So in this area, I'm Cap'n Dell to everybody. Now that I'm on-line, it has really spread out - not in importance, but in miles. I have sent messages all over the United States and some overseas, using that name. I like the name, also, and I'm glad that Clyde gave it to me.

LIFE BACK THEN

Growing Up in Hobucken

I grew up in Hobucken, North Carolina, a small fishing village of four hundred on an island on Jones Bay on the South End of Goose Creek Island. We had almost everything we needed to survive: a big garden (we did a lot of canning during the summer), fig bushes, grapevines, and apple trees. There were six operating stores in the community; we did buy flour, and our primary income came from fishing in the summer and oystering in the winter. We were a typical fishing family, as were most all that lived here.

We had about six acres of tillable farmland; we grew the corn for the stock to eat. We had one mule, a cow, chickens and hogs, and a good warm home to live in, surrounded by plenty of family love. My world was small, about one mile each way of my home. I walked to school and came home for a dinner of collards and pigtails, seafood, or chicken, and molasses and cream with a biscuit. We had good teachers and class-mates. They were all about like me; their world was this island. For the most part, we were happy with our surroundings.

We played at the boat landing where all the boats tied up. Usually, there would be a group of men there. When word came into our community about a boat that had broken loose from its moorings or was sunk, every-body went to the creek to offer help. We went swimming every day during the summer; sometimes we might go two or three times.

One day was set aside for the community to go and clean up the cemetery. Usually there was a good crowd; there was a lot of talking going on between older folks, finding out about the sick, and other things going on.

We all went to church on Sunday; nobody was asked if they were going, you just went. (There wasn't much sinning going on - the worst you could do was to steal a watermelon or an apple off someone's tree.) I didn't mind going; it gave you a chance to mingle and play with the girls, and usually this was the biggest group of folks getting together at one time. There was a lot of praying by the old folks for those that needed help.

We had homecomings - "dinner on the ground," as it was called. Everyone around attended this, regardless of where they may have gone to church normally.

We always had a Christmas Eve service. Old Santa Claus would arrive and go around to greet us children, and then set up by the big Christmas tree in the front of the church. It was the most beautiful sight I ever saw, and this was truly the most looked-for event of the year. When it was time to go home, we were given an orange and an apple on the way out. In later years (1945-50), the classes went to drawing names and exchanging presents; this also added something to the service.

I can remember seeing those old men working on the church building, doing what was necessary to keep it in good shape. Occasionally, there would be a house moving and everybody would help get it to where it was to go.

I think we were a caring community; everybody knew of others' needs and, one way or the other, came to their aid. This was the most enjoyable time in my entire life. I will remember it as long as I'm able.

Going to the Movies at Aurora

One of the earliest and fondest memories I have is going to the movies at Aurora. It was always on Saturday night, and a western. This was different; a change from the normal of just going to school and playing with friends here in the community - a chance to go to town.

Mr. Oscar Barnett and his family, who lived on the Lowland road, got to going to Aurora in their car every Saturday night. After a few times going, he found out there were some other people that would like to go. He was a farmer, and he and his daddy had a sawmill not far from their house, which is the reason he had a two-ton truck. The truck had four-foot sides on it, and the front was closed off, so he went to driving in on Saturday night, leaving home about six o'clock to make the seven o'clock movie.

He would come around by the school to the corner. (The corner, as it was called then, is where the schoolhouse road and Rt. 304 meet - there were two stores there at that time.) Some of us would be there by three o'clock to make sure we didn't miss him. He charged a quarter to take you to Aurora, and the price of a movie ticket was eighteen cents, so you needed forty-three cents to make it. Sometimes, we would have to take some eggs to the store and sell them to get enough money to go.

It wasn't long before that truck would be full of people when it left the corner - whole families going, and a lot of just mothers and children. The War was going on, and the fathers were in the service. They would put us children in the front, and the men would be across the back. These trips were the first place I was allowed to go by myself. I'm sure Mama felt it was safe, or I wouldn't have gone.

In the summertime, when the days were long, it would still be light going over. Those women would break out and start singing, and soon everybody would join in, songs that were popular, like "Buttons and Bows", "South of the Border"," Don't Fence Me In", and there were others, as well as church hymns. These were happy people, as I look at it now. Mr. Barnett had a tarp back of his seat that was used if the weather was bad. In the winter, he would wrap the whole back of the truck up, so we could be warm.

When we got to Aurora, he would park close to where Mr. Jasper Mill's old shop is. We would unload and head towards the theater. You could hardly walk, for people. The streets were full of people from one end of Aurora to the other. It was like this: all seemed to be happy, all the shops were open - even Dr. Bonner would be sitting out in front of this office, if nobody was sick and needed him.

When we got to the theater, there would be a line at the ticket office. After you got your ticket and got inside, boy, you felt like this was the

13

place to be on Saturday night - there was nothing quite like it anyplace. Most of the time, the theater was full ten minutes before time for the movie to begin, and people were standing in the back.

After the movie was over, we would head back to the truck to head back home, thinking that now the world was a safer place. After all, we had just seen a lot of bad guys locked up; it had to be.

Sometimes when he headed home, you could tell that probably everybody didn't go to the movie. Some of the men seemed to be a little happier on the way back than when we went over. Their talking was much louder, and there was more of it - some of the things they talked about were funny.

Those were the good, old days if there ever was any, but time moved on and buses came about. Mr. Clyde Jones and his wife, Ms. Ivy, started running a bus - which wasn't enough - so they bought three more: one going to Bayboro, and the other three going to Aurora. They were hauling out of Lowland, also, and they were all full. It was a happy time for everybody.

People were allowed to catch oysters by using powerboats, so there was more money around, and you could tell it on Saturday nights. This was a time in my life I don't want to forget.

Making Home-Style Molasses

One of the things that the old folks did was to make molasses from the cane that they grew in their fields. We sopped it up with hot Mama-made biscuits and rich cow's cream poured over it – yum, yum.

Most of the time, the whole community was involved in the process. It took all day and several different steps to get it to the barrel it was stored in. There were two cane mills on the Island. Mr. John Carawan had the first one at his home in Lowland, and later on, Mr. Herbert

Pollard, Mr. Joseph Roberson, and Mr. Edmond Jones owned one together in Hobucken. It was on the School House Road on Mr. Herbert Pollard's land; Mr. Joseph Robertson was the cooker. His son, Bert, and Mary Alice Spain both told me they had had their fingers burned many times sampling the molasses. (They lived close to where it was going on.)

People set aside a portion of their land to grow the cane. It looked a lot like corn; it was about the same size in height and width, but the tassel (or seedpod) was different. When it was ripe and ready, the first thing they had to do was strip all the leaves from it while it was still standing in the field. Then it was cut and hauled to the boiling site, where the top was cut off. This is where other people got involved in the process; others came just to see what was going on.

The stalks were then ready to run through the cane mill. This was quite an operation. The cane mill was a set of rollers set close together in a frame with gears on top and a pan with a spout underneath. One of the shafts went on up fairly high and had another bracket on it. This was where a pole was attached, about twelve feet in length running off clear of the mill. The mule that had hauled cane in the cart to the site was unhooked, and the pole from the cane mill was hooked behind him in about the same place as the plow had been. (Sometimes there was a special mule there, because not all mules understood what they were supposed to do.)

The mule walked around in a circle, turning the mill as he went. There was a rope hooked to his bridle bit that went to where the pole hooked to the machine. It was tight enough to keep him from trying to get away; his instinct was to move away from it. There was a person working under the pole, feeding the cane into the mill and making sure not to put too much into it because the mule would stop if it got too hard to pull. He also had to make sure the bucket was in the right place to catch the liquid as it was squeezed out of the stalks. It was pea green sweet juice, and watery; the flies were attracted to it.

Close by was a big pan called the boiler pan. It was about seven feet long, three feet wide, and six inches deep, and would hold seventy-five to a hundred gallons. It had partitions in it that reached from one side almost to the other, and made the juice zigzag as it went down the pan. You needed plenty of long firewood under the pan, and lots of manpower. First, a hot fire was built under it from one end to the other, and then the juice was brought from the bucket under the mill. On the way, it was poured through big cloths to filter out any trash that had gotten into it. Pouring the juice into the pan was a six-to- seven-hour job; as the juice began to boil, it had to be constantly skimmed to remove the cane residue that rises to the top. Small paddles were used to keep it moving until it was "ready", as they called it. Mary Alice said her folks made her her own little paddle so she could help.

There was great skill involved in knowing when it was the right time to stop cooking it: if all the water wasn't removed, it would turn sour and be no good; if it was overcooked, it would have a burnt taste and turn to sugar.

I had the pleasure of going over to Aurora and sitting with Mr. Charles Carawan and his wife Mabel recently. They were both borne in Lowland; he is the son of Mr. John Carawan who had the cane mill at his house from 1928-30. Charles told me that the family that brought the cane in operated the mill to get the juice, and his father cooked it for them. He was paid with a portion of the molasses. One year, they had plenty of molasses and one of the barrels soured, so they had to get rid of it. Mr. John had about a dozen hogs in a pen and decided to feed it to them. Not knowing what was about to happen, Charles said his daddy put some of the molasses out and came back into the house. In a little while, the hogs became noisy, which was unusual. They were squealing real loud, so he went out to the pen. Some of the hogs were setting just like a dog, shaking their heads and squealing; some were lying down and squealing, and Charles said some of them were actually smiling. The juice had fermented and the hogs were drunk.

16

Another story was told to me by Mrs. Joannie Spain. She said that one day, a bunch of children were playing when the word came out that they were making molasses through the swamp, a distance of about a mile. The children went and got cold biscuits and went through there, and sopped the molasses up as they made it. It was just like a Camp Meeting day, she said.

I have tried to trace down these machines, and had about given up on finding either one of them. Then I had some pretty good luck. I was in Charlie's Restaurant and Bill Potter and his wife Wayne Ray and their son, Grady, were at another table. They stopped by at our table on their way out. In the conversation, I asked Bill what he knew about making molasses. He said he knew quite a bit and that he had Mr. Edgar Barnett's machine. It was the machine that was here in Hobucken and Mr. Edgar Barnett got it; he lived up the Springs Creek Road between Lowland and Hobucken, and made molasses with it. (I don't think he made any more than for his own use.) After Mr. Edgar got old enough so that he couldn't get his driver's license renewed, he went around on his tractor until that gave out. Bill Potter from Lowland saw the problem and went to stopping by on his way out and picking Mr. Edgar up so he could get whatever they needed.

One day, Mr. Edgar told Bill that he could have the old mill and pan, so Bill got it. Bill told me he had planned to grow cane and make some molasses from it, but it never happened. The old mill was put in a building and kept inside until the storms of 1999 took the building down.

There are still a lot of these mills around; they are turned by an engine of some kind. I'm told they still make molasses in the mountains, too, and that it's a tourist attraction in some places.

Old Folks Moving

With today's modern transportation being like it is, all we have to do is walk out and get into our car or truck and drive wherever we want to go. It is easy to move from one area to another using our own vehicles. If a job is too big, or we are moving a long distance, we call a moving company to come and load up our possessions and they take them where we tell them to go.

Most everything that is moved is inside the house. There might be a swing set or something like that outside, and sometimes it is left there. People just get a new one if it's still needed at the new location.

We think back in time and most of us just assume that everybody stayed pretty close to where they were raised up; that they didn't move much because of the difficulties involved and the way they had to do it. But we are wrong; the old folks would move in a heartbeat. They used a mule and cart, if it was a move from one place to another in the community; skiffs and sailboats were used if it was to another area. If the house belonged to them and they wanted to take it, they dropped it down on skids and rollers, and took a stump puller with a mule hooked to it so that as he went around and around, he pulled it towards it.

I saw a house on rollers being moved when I was a small boy; they came up the road with it. I have been told that in some cases the house couldn't be moved because of the distance, so they would take it down piece by piece, load it up on mule and cart, and haul it to the new site or creek and put it on a boat. Once they got all the pieces there, they would put it back together and move in. They moved a lot of houses this way.

I have several different copies of estate sales from 1800 to 1850. Most of the items sold were kitchen utensils, a table and chairs, a chair or two from the room they set in, a couple of featherbeds and bedsteads, and always a chest where all the valuables were kept. That wasn't that many things to move from inside the house.

The animals that lived on the outside were a different story. They were sometimes sold or given away as they were, wherever they were. (At the estate sale of William A. Spain at Lowland in 1847, his dry cow was sold for twelve dollars. The cow was in Piney Woods, according to the paper.) When old folks moved from one place to another within the community, they would walk, but moving to another area was a different problem if they decided to take some of the livestock with them. They would catch the chickens and tie their legs together, so they could get a hold of them when the time came. Sam Swindell said that his granddaddy moved so many times (four times in one week), they didn't untie the chickens' legs for a week.

The mule and hogs could be left for a few days; they would get somebody to look after them until they could come back for them. The cow was a different thing; it had to be taken along with the family for two reasons: it needed to be milked every day, and most important, if there were children in the family, they needed the milk to drink and the cow was where it was stored. They did have places they could set the milk in and let it sour, turn to clabber, and then eat it, but not while they were moving.

I got with some older people a few days ago, and we got to talking about how and why the old folks moved so much. Most of them said they had no way to get to their jobs, so if there was a vacant house close by, they would move into it until they got the job done. If a better house became vacant while they were doing the job, they would move again. Sometimes the rent would come due, and that would be another reason to move.

According to my older brother and sisters, my family wasn't any different. They moved to Oriental in 1920. Daddy had bought a home here in Hobucken (my home place), and was hauling freight for Mr. Rufus Alcock on the bateau Neptune.

He quit, and got a job hauling fish from the pound netters at Brant Island to Oriental for Else Goodwin, who lived at Oriental. To come to Hobucken from that route was quite a long distance out of the way, so he and my mama closed everything up here and went to Oriental. They rented the upstairs in what was called the Purdy Building. (The Holly and Ivy shop is in that building today, across the street from the Civic Center on the same side.)

My folks don't remember much about moving up there, but they remember a whole lot about moving back. With three small children and a baby, climbing up those stairs got to Mama pretty quick, what with knowing that their home here in Hobucken was empty.

In a few months, the job was over for the year and my family decided to move back. It was just after Christmas and cold. Daddy borrowed the Neptune from Mr. Ruff and went to Oriental with it.

The next morning, they loaded up everything to come back, including the cow. They said it wasn't too bad that morning. Uncle Fred had just got back from Europe, where he was in the First World War, and went to help them. The boat had an engine in it, but they couldn't get it running. While one person worked on it, the other was polling because there wasn't enough wind to use the sails. Just before sundown, a cold front came across and it went to turning cold. They were at the mouth of Broad Creek, so they went into the public dock at Whortonsville. (Every community had a public dock so the freight boats could tie up and load poultry and produce and anything else that needed to go to the market, and bring back things that the stores and folks had ordered.)

Mr. Eugene Lupton lived close to the dock. He came down and invited Mama to come up with the kids and spend the night with his folks. (Mr. Eugene was also Sheriff of the county at that time.) Valeria said when they got ready to go to bed, those featherbeds were the biggest she ever saw; they sure slept well that night.

Daddy and Uncle Fred didn't have it as good. Just after dark, it went to sleeting and snowing, and about every four hours they had to pump the boat out. The snow and ice went to building up on the cow. She was standing up on deck, so Daddy got the tablecloth out and tied it around her to help keep her warm. They didn't get much sleep, on account of the weather and pumping the boat out.

The next morning, the weather was still bad; it had quit snowing, but the wind was blowing hard and it was very cold.

My older brother and sisters don't know where Daddy or Mr. Eugene Lupton called in Oriental, but the word got there about them. Mr. Dave Wilkerson operated a new powerboat and he came to Whortonsville. They loaded everything on his boat - including the cow - and headed down Neuse River. It was rough; Mama and the kids got inside the cabin where it was warm. What with the smell of the engine fumes and the boat rolling, Valeria got seasick. She said it was the first time she had experienced anything like it.

They finally got home okay. After that experience, Daddy and Mama never moved again. They finished out their lives in the home here in Hobucken.

This was told to me by my older brother and sisters; it was three more babies, and about ten years later, before I came into the world. Things were better for everybody by that time.

Fellowship in the Outhouse

It seems that the fellowship that existed between family members years ago is not here today. With everybody working and doing their own thing, they have no time for one another, especially between mother, father, and children. Today, no one talks much; everyone's looking at television, playing Nintendo, or going to bed.

This is a story about people who were born before 1945 and raised up in the country, with the outhouse out back in full use; and the fellowship that went on in the family home place in every area of life. The outhouse was a part of life; it was kept in good shape and no wood around the bottom could be rotten. Most of the time you could tell how many people were in the family by looking at the size of it. Two holes were standard - one small hole and a bigger one. There were three, as well as four, holes in use, also. The older folk had some ideas about making them more attractive - they would put lilies around them, those orange lilies that grow almost anywhere they hit the ground. They were referred to as "outhouse lilies".

When we were little - from about five to ten-years old - we started school and met new friends and just enjoyed playing with them so much, we didn't want to stop to take care of our own bodily functions during the daylight hours, so we waited. (Every animal of every species has these functions, humans included; it's a very natural part of living.)

About sundown, after all the playing had stopped and you went into the house for supper and sitting around talking with other family members, the urge to take care of the bodily function got greater, so you had to do something about it. It was too early to use the pot that sits in the bedrooms; you use them at bedtime and later. At night, you were scared to go to the outhouse because it was dark, so someone bigger had to go with you. The father or older boys went with the little boys, and the mother or older girls went with the little girls. A big advantage of going at night was that you didn't have to close the door. Sitting there with a bright full moon - so you could see everything - was an enjoyable time.

In my home, it was my father who went with me most of the time, when he was home. Having him go was a real pleasure; there were no questions out of range about the things on earth or seas or the stars in heaven, that couldn't be answered. After all, you were sitting there with the smartest person on earth. Most always, the toilet was in the fenced-in area where the stock of every kind was kept. This usually joined the house lot (but was not too close to the house) so that all the land that could be farmed was used to grow crops. They were two or three different size holes for most families, depending on what size you needed as you aged.

The conversation usually went like this when you had set down and now it was time to talk. "Daddy, the cow and old Bill (mule) are looking at us. Can they see us in here?" He would say, "Yes, they can see us. Animals can see as well at night as they can in the daytime." "Old Bill is coming over. Is he coming in here with us?" "No, he's coming over to look at us. He will stop when he gets close. He likes us. He's hoping we have got some food for him." "Will the cow come over too?" "She might," he says. "She likes us too, and that's where we get our milk." "Daddy, I see the chickens go into the chicken house every evening at sundown and go to sleep, but I can hear those sounds like little chips. Are they asleep?" He says, "Yes, they make those sounds during the night. They can get real noisy if a varmint gets in there. They will be flying everywhere. They can't see too well at night. They will get eaten up if they don't get out of the way, so they make a noise to alert the others of the danger in the chicken house. Usually, we can hear them and we run out here to see what is wrong, and fix it."

"The hogs are over in the corner in a pen," I say. "Why are they over there? They don't make much noise." "We usually keep them away from the house. They like to roll in the mud and they have a bad smell and the flies get bad." "Do we eat them?" "Yes, that's where the ham, bacon, and sausage we eat comes from. But don't worry, at hog-killing time, they're hung up on a scaffold and cleaned real good with hot scalding water poured over them. All the meat is smoked and cured to keep it from spoiling."

"I see the moon and a whole wide space of stars," I say. "Is the moon made of cheese? It looks like it." "I don't know, it might be. There are faces on it sometimes that you can see. The sun shines on it - that makes it shine like it does. There are some people that have looked at it through a telescope and they say it looks like there are rocks on it, but no clouds or rain. Nobody has never been to the moon, so there's not much known about it. It moves every night to a different place. We plant our crops

23

when the moon is right and a whole lot of other things are done by look-ing and seeing if the moon is in the right place."

"There are some big stars and some little stars," he says. "Some look close and some a long way off." "What do they do? What holds them up there?" "Here on earth, we don't know much about all the stars. You see, they're used to navigate ships by on the oceans, and there is a star - or stars - that come up before daylight and go right up over the North Star. We can't see it now... it doesn't move like the others do." "Daddy, there is a little bunch of stars up there that looks like a little pot with a handle on it ...do you see it?" "Yes, I see it. It's called the Little Dipper. There is another one that's bigger than this one... it's called the Big Dipper. We can see it from here. The Old Testament tells a lot about the stars and we have to remember that those stars are not controlled by anybody on this earth. We have to leave that up to the Lord; he's in charge of the heavens and we just have to trust him and leave it up to him. Nothing will be out of place with him in control." "If I was anywhere else on earth or sea, could I see the stars and moon there, too?" "Yes, they may be in different places in the sky, but they are for everybody."

After the job is done, we get the catalog out (an improvement over the corncob). We use the thin, black and white pages first - those real pretty, colorful pages are used as a last resort. They are too thick and too slick to get the job done. When this is done, you head on back into the house where the rest of the family is sitting and talking.

When you come in, you see a pan of warm water and soap and Mama waiting to give you your bath and put your pajamas on to get ready for bed. After you have had a chance to sit and talk to the other family members for a while, Mama takes a lamp and tells you to come on, it's bedtime.

After you get tucked in and get a goodnight hug and kiss, you know how much you have learned today and that you are loved, because you can feel it. You are so glad to be in this world, because you are a special person - loved by everybody, and the whole world is good; nothing could be wrong with such good people that I know.

And you go to sleep; not a worry in the mind, everything is lovely. It's good to go back and relive these times in our minds, but I believe I will stay with the indoor plumbing of today. I didn't mention the times when it was about thirty degrees outside, or very hot, with mosquitoes biting and spiders and snakes crawling. Those weren't the best of times, in this situation.

I guess in a lot of places - our country and all over the world - these outhouses are still in use by a lot of people, especially when there are wars going on.

To the people who read my stories - this is our history and I have been working on it for a long time. All of the folks that were living when I retired are no longer with us. When I get an idea about a story, there is no one to ask. I'm the old one now.

Baseball in the Twenties

Baseball is big business today - big salaries and super stars, and all the glitter that goes with it. People still get excited about it and plan all of the week's activities so that on the weekend, everything comes to a halt on Saturday and Sunday evenings so they can be in their living rooms to see the games - sometimes with two or three televisions on in order to watch more games at the same time. I have seen some folks cut the television off; it makes them so mad when it's not going their way.

Some of the people I meet during the week talk a lot about the games. We may not agree with some of the calls that are made, and slip out on the front edge of our sofas and recliners to talk to the television set - wanting to see an instant replay quickly, and telling the set how it should have been called.

We all have our favorite drinks and popcorn, potato chips, coffee, cakes, and ice cream while the games are going on, and now we know what these couch potatoes are all about. This is the kind of game we play today, and it's what we do best.

It's not always been this way. People years ago enjoyed ball games and would lay out their work in order to play ball or see the games on the weekends. There were two things that the old folks took serious: ball games and politics.

The games weren't in the living rooms - you had to go out to the ball diamond in order to see or play ball. People would set on the grass around the field or under a tree, if there was any close. A lot of family get-togethers happened at these games, and it gave the children a chance to run and play and meet new friends. A lot of socializing went on at these games.

Ever since I can remember, baseball has been around. I played some in the late fifties and sixties. It was an enjoyable game, especially when you were winning. We didn't have two hundred bats to choose from, or a new ball with every pitch - we had about five bats and one ball and a spare, if it was needed. Sometimes you could see the water fly when it was hit, it would be so wet.

The ball was changed when the cover was coming off. No ground-rule doubles or anything else like they have today. We played the best we could and batted the ball when it came our time to bat. And when we caught the ball, the batter was out. There were times when everything didn't go smoothly. You could see tempers flare and fists balled up and people ready to fight over a play that was called. I have heard where there were some clothes torn off at some of these games. I never saw it while I played.

Baseball got real popular in the forties, with games played by the women, as well as the men. There would be two games played both days - the women first, and then the men. One time at Lowland, the women were playing and one of the umpires for the game was the husband of one of them. He was calling third base. His wife was coming around to third base and the ball was coming too, so he had to make a call, and he called his wife out on the play. She didn't agree with the call, and proceeded to tell him about it. He didn't change his call, and as she headed in, she turned around and in a loud voice told him to just wait until they got home - he would find out who was out. I didn't hear any more about it.

There were some young men up the prong at Lowland that played ball just about all the time. Two of those men I've heard of over the years were Tommie Guy McKinney and Denard Carawan. I have heard my daddy say that Denard Carawan could run the fastest of anybody he ever saw. He was a good baseball player. When he got his eye on the ball, nothing got in his way, and most of the time he got it; he was a man who liked the game. Other people have told me the same thing about Denard. These men that were playing could have been a big influence on Bones McKinney and his career; in the early years of his life, Bones was among these folks.

Walter Sadler told me that he was on a baseball team about 1924, made up with Carawans from up the prong at Lowland and other folks from the island. There were other teams around the county that they played almost all the time.

Walter Sadler

Walter said they got word that a team at Whortonsville wanted to play them, and they decided to go over. When the day came, they went by boat across Bay River, up Bonner's Bay to Florence. Somebody picked them up (he doesn't remember who) and took them on over to Whortonsville.

The diamond was laid out on the side of a creek and it was all right to play on. When the time came to start the game, everybody was ready. There were a lot of people there to watch it.

Walter told me that he was playing third base and Denard was in the outfield. They had been playing awhile. Whortonsville was ahead - he doesn't remember how much – and the crowd that was there was doing a lot of hollering. It seemed they were all enjoying the game.

Eugene Lupton was a big boy growing up - very strong, and a powerful hitter when he came to bat. He was playing for Whortonsville. (He went on to become the sheriff of the county.)

Denard Carawan

Eugene came to bat and the pitch was just right for him. He hit it very hard; everybody knew it was going in the creek, and the crowd went wild, jumping up and down, waving their hats, and dancing around. Eugene heard them and turned his head towards the crowd, took off his hat, and went to waving it as he trotted and skipped along around the bases. It was a nice hit, but Denard had got his eye on the ball. It was headed into the field. He went to running to get under it, and when he got to the side of the creek he didn't stop - he went right on into the creek and was there when it came down.

Eugene was looking towards the crowd and all of a sudden everything went quiet. He hollered towards the crowd, "did he catch that d---- ball?" The crowd said "yes," Eugene turned around, and Denard was coming out of the creek with the ball in his glove.

You will never see a play like that on television because that would be an automatic home run in today's game. We hear a lot about family entertainment today on the tube. The folks had it back then, but it was out at the community ball diamonds. Walter said it didn't change anything, they still got beat.

You can tell that Walter enjoys being there as he tells about this game.

The Lowland Homecoming

This was the first event I can remember going to here on the Island, other than school and church. I don't remember how we got there; we had no car, so I guess we either went with someone else, or by boat to Eastman's Creek and walked up to the church. I do remember that there were a lot of people there. I didn't pay much attention to the speeches that were made, but there were a lot of new kids to play with I had never met before.

Just north of the church, a platform with rails had been built about twenty-feet square for the speakers, and there was a high school band from Belhaven there to play.

All the band players were dressed in red and white uniforms. They were very impressive to look at, and they introduced me to a type of music I hadn't heard before. Needless to say, it wasn't my kind of music. I liked the hillbilly music that Mama and Daddy played from the radio at about four o'clock in the morning, as Daddy got ready to get off to work.

The below item was taken from the *New Bern Tribune* dated Sept 5, 1939, written by Billy Auther.

THREE THOUSAND ATTEND LOWLAND HOMECOMING
Rep. Graham A. Barden, House Speaker D. L. Ward, Among Speakers for the First Annual Event

Three thousand persons attended the First Annual Goose Creek Island homecoming at Lowland Sunday and heard Rep. Graham A. Barden call for a building up of resistance against war.

The throng (many of them were former residents of Pamlico County and the Island) came from as far away points as New York, Connecticut, and Florida.

WARD SPEAKS

House Speaker D. L. Ward told the gathering that it is "only through the home - and spirit of the home - that we can preserve the ideals of this great democracy. And if Mr. Barden does his best to keep us out of war, then I'll make my best efforts to get the Cash Corner - Hobucken - Lowland road paved."

The road from Cash Corner to Hobucken was in exceptionally bad condition Sunday. Many Pamlicoans chose to go by Aurora, rather than brave the muddy stretch that had been under construction more than a year. Several cars nearly got stuck in several deep mud holes along the route.

MASTER OF CEREMONIES

Kelly Watson, prominent Lowland seafood dealer, was master of ceremonies. Others on the program were: J. W. McLeary of Jacksonville, who delivered the early devotional, and Rev. R. B. Spencer of Ayden, who spoke on "Home Here"; H. B. Carawan and Rev. J. R. Lee of Washington, who delivered the welcome and response; Billy Arthur, New Bern newspaperman; the Belhaven brass band; and the Lowland choir.

Mr. Barden deplored the idea he said was current - that the United States could not keep out of a European war - and the tendency of Americans to ask if the United States will become involved.

U.S. "CAN" STAY OUT

"I see no reason to go into it; we can't afford to go into it; we must not go into it; and I don't think we will go into it," Mr. Barden declared.
He asked why the United States should enter the "tragedy" and jeopardize its own ideals. "We still have the cripples, widows, and orphans, of the last war with us," he said, "and let that be a gentle reminder when we say we can't stay out of the war . . . Let's be slow about poking our necks out far enough to get in someone else's war."

Will Enlist

"As I've said before, the day I vote to plunge America into war is the day I'll present myself to the recruiting station for enlistment."

Members of the choir were: Mrs. Mary Henries, Mrs. Nelia Watson, Mrs. Catherine Ireland, Warden Lewis, Mrs. Allie Potter, Mrs. Adelaide Ross, William Henries, Buel Potter, Alvin Henries, George Daniels, William Thomas Campen, Marvin Potter and Miss Myra Sawyer, pianist.

Hog Killing Time

Back in the 30's and 40's around Thanksgiving time, people went to getting ready to kill hogs. You could tell by the preparations that were going on - wash pots were being borrowed and set in place; a scaffold would be borrowed or built to hang the hogs on after they were shot and stuck in the throat, so they could continue to be cleaned; tables were set up to work on and cut the meat when the time came for that.

At daybreak on the day chosen, the pots were filled with water and the wood was put under and around the pots to get the water real hot. It took a lot of hot water and a lot of good grade wood to keep the fires going all day.

We had an old white mule. We called him Old Bill, and he had a mind of his own. From way back, I would hear Daddy and Uncle Fred Spain talk about how bad he was to work. If Old Bill decided he wasn't going to do something, it was just about impossible to get him to do it. And when you came to a bridge in the road, he would stop. When he decided to go across, he would try to jump it.

One time my older brother Thomas was hauling wood with Old Bill and the mule jumped the cart in the ditch, breaking one of the shafts off. They had to borrow a cart to finish with. Uncle Fred had an old 1928 Chevrolet truck in his yard and he wanted to move it, so they hooked Old

Bill to it. When the rope came tight he would stop. He wouldn't pull on it, and they couldn't make him do it, so they had to move it another way. They put him back into the pound.

We were getting ready to kill hogs one year and Daddy needed some wood, so he and Uncle Fred hooked Old Bill to the cart to go down in Drum Creek Swamp to get some. I was probably about five years old, so he took me with him. We had a dog named Sparkey and he went also - sometimes he rode in the cart with us.

We went right on down the road, almost to the second bridge below Hobucken, and turned left off the main road in the marsh, going over to what is called "the six foot ditch" that went from the head of Drum Creek, on up into the woods. When we got to this ditch, we followed it. After we got in the woods, Daddy tied Old Bill to a tree and he and Uncle Fred started to gathering and putting the wood in a pile. When they had gotten all there was in that area, Daddy came and got Old Bill by the bridle and led him over and backed him up to the pile. I was still in the cart holding onto the boards that went across the front of the cart and the dog was in there with me.

Daddy and Uncle Fred throwed what they had gotten in the cart, but Daddy needed a little bit more, so he took Old Bill and led him back out to the side of the ditch and tied him to something, and went on back in the woods to get enough wood to finish loading the cart.

After Daddy and Uncle Fred had worked awhile, for some reason, Old Bill decided he wanted to go home. He pulled his bridle loose, and started turning around and backing up. He backed the cart in the ditch, dumping all the wood and the dog in the cart out. I saw what was going to happen, and I was old enough to know to get ahold of the front of the cart, so I went to hollering for Daddy. He heard me, and came running. We had gone quite a ways before he stopped Old Bill. I thought he was going to hit him with a stick, but he didn't - he did hit him about the head with his hat. Then he turned Old Bill around and we headed back. The wood that was in the ditch was under the water, so it wasn't any good. They continued gathering wood and we finally got home about sundown. I head Daddy talking to Old Bill as he fed him. It still wasn't good, but by bedtime I could tell he was not upset anymore, and Old Bill continued to be Old Bill.

Babe Ruth and Max Lanier at Hobucken

December 7th - a day that's very famous in American history - was a day that affected many lives and the direction of our country in world history. Of course, I'm writing about the Japanese attack on Pearl Harbor.

We had another event that caused a lot of excitement here on Goose Creek Island that happened on Dec. 7, but it was 1931 rather than 1941: Babe Ruth came here to go duck hunting with Mr. Ralph and Mr. Harmon Mayo, known among hunters as the Mayo brothers.

Mr. Ralph operated a store and took out people who wanted to go hunting. He loved to hunt, and would close the store up when it came to hunting time. The old store building he operated is still standing here in the west end of Hobucken. The Mayo brothers married Ms. Ada and Ms. Ruth Whorton from Whortonsville, sisters who taught school many years here at Hobucken. It was a very busy time of the year during hunting season.

Babe Ruth had been in Craven County hunting quail and dove in the Catfish Lake area with Mr. Scott, who operated an oil company in New Bern. Babe Ruth wanted to go duck hunting before he went back to New York. It was decided to call the Mayo Brothers and ask them if they would take them out to their blinds for a day of hunting.

Mr. Ralph told them they would - to be there the next morning about an hour before daylight to get started. This time of the year, Ms. Ada and Ms. Ruth got up at 4 A.M. to prepare breakfast and make sandwiches for them to take with them. Sometimes they had to have help, and there were several different women from here in the community that helped them.

Babe Ruth and Mr. Herman, who was sportswriter for the New York Yankees, showed up the next morning. It was a cold morning; a good day for duck hunting, and they soon left to go out. When they got to the blinds and got set up, the canvasbacks and redheads were really flying good, and they began to shoot. Capt. Ralph was considered to be one of the best around with a gun. Babe Ruth was said to be good, too. Pretty soon, there was a shooting contest going on between them. Mrs. Ruth said she thought Capt. Ralph won. The limit was thirty ducks, and Babe Ruth had no trouble getting his.

During the day, the word got out here on the Island about Babe Ruth being here with the Mayo brothers. There was a big crowd at the store when he and his party returned that night.

Ms. Ruth and Ms. Ada said he had such a nice and warm personality and was interested in talking to the people, especially the young folks. They said you couldn't forget such a person as he was. Carl Alcock said Babe Ruth patted him on the shoulder and told him he would be all right. (Carl was interested in talking to him about baseball.) Babe Ruth wrote in his diary that it was a most enjoyable day.

In 1939, another famous baseball player to come to Hobucken was Max Lanier, the great left-handed pitcher for the Cardinals. He came with his brother, Ray, from Denton, N. C., to go deer hunting with the Mayo brothers and stayed with Mrs. Ada and Mr. Harmon for about three days in their home. Mrs. Ada said that she and Mr. Harmon were concerned about the mosquitoes when he came. Max told them that he knew about the mosquitoes; he had encountered them around in different parts of the country, and was prepared for them. He had hats with nets over them and protective overalls for their bodies.

They had very good luck deer hunting, and seemed very excited with everything. They fit in real well. After they had eaten the evening meal, Max would take his guitar - which he could play very well - and go over to Ralph's store and play and sing for all the folks that had gathered there just to get a chance to meet him. He would ask if anybody had a request, and if he knew it, he would do it for them. Most of the time, all the hunters from the area would be there; usually the store was full. Mr. Lanier came down three years in a row. There were other hunters of lesser fame who came down to hunt, and they received the same hospitality.

Mrs. Ada and Mrs. Ruth Mayo said their standard breakfast was grapefruit first, then ham and fried or scrambled eggs, grits or rice, hot biscuits and coffee, and a serving of good hospitality. This wasn't McDonald's or Hardees; it was the old-fashioned way. They would pre-pare sandwiches for the men to take with them and eat during the day. After all this was done and cleaned up, they went and taught school all day at the schoolhouse. Most every-body who went to this school was in their class at some time.

Mrs. Ada Wharton Mayo

When Mrs. Ada and Mrs. Ruth Mayo got back home, they had to pre-pare the evening meal, which most of the time consisted of seafood, country home-cooked vegetables, cornbread and coffee. Dessert was chocolate or lemon pie, and more good hospitality. The hunters expressed great delight about the food. They would tell the ladies that they were looking forward to the good meals as much as the hunting, and they left very generous tips. The ladies put in long days in order to get all this done.

I've been talking with them about this story for six months or more, but in the last three months our church group and pastor have been going to their house. After having a little prayer session with them, I take my guitar and we sing them a few songs, have communion with them, and enjoy being in their company. It is such a joy, just to hear them talk about their lives. One of the ladies in our group told them that they didn't know of anybody who had touched and helped form as many lives as they had. I heard Mrs. Ada tell Mrs. Annie Goodwin that she had taught her when she was in the first grade at Whortonsville. Mrs. Annie is seventy-eight now.

There are nine of us in my family, and I guess Mrs. Ruth started all of us in the first grade. Mrs. Ada began teaching in 1921 and retired in 1962. Mrs. Ruth started in 1923 and retired in 1962. It is a pleasure to be in the company of these fine ladies

Roy Watson

Something for everybody: this story is for the hunters and sportsman of the area about how hunting was done sixty years ago. I hadn't written one for this group of people before.

My Education at Hobucken High School

My education got off to a rocky start. It was an uphill battle from the very beginning: a head tide all the way. I started school in 1937. My birthday being on October 7 (and the cut-off day October 1), I needed six days to make me six years old; Mama sent me anyhow. Coming from a big family, I guess one of the first things you learn is how to look after yourself. Probably the first or second day of school, I'm sure I was showing off a little and needed some correction. Mrs. Ruth Mayo was the teacher and when she came over to correct me, I reached up and slapped her. I finished out that day but, when I got home, Mama had already gotten word to keep me home another year. I never knew whether it was because of my actions, or because I wasn't old enough; Mrs. Ruth says she doesn't remember. I started the next year with Mrs. Ruth, and we got along fine.

I don't remember much about the second grade, except that our teacher was Mrs. McCleese. I remember the third grade well - Mrs. White was our teacher and Mr. Chadwick was the Principal and he was boarding with us. This was the year the school burned down. Sometime during the year, they started to cleaning up the mess - there was a big pile of old tin, bricks, glass, rocks and other things at each end of where the old building had been. These piles had been roped off and a sign put up telling us to keep out. But one day they were just ignored, and some older boys got to throwing whatever was handy. Then they would run to the back of these piles for protection, with more boys joining all the time. We had from twelve to one off for lunch; I could come home, eat, and be back to school in forty minutes. This day when I got back out there, there were about a dozen boys on each end and there was almost a war going on. I could hardly wait to get into it. I had just got in there and had a small rock ready to throw, when I heard a voice telling me to drop it. It was Mr. Chadwick. Mrs. Banks was at the other pile, rounding the boys up. We were told to go to Mr. Chadwick's office.

When the office was full, Mr. Chadwick told everybody to line up, with the biggest first and the smallest last, which was me. Then he went to using that paddle and I can tell you - he was cutting them no slack. When he got done, they were ready to go out of that door. My brother Charles was just ahead of me in line. I'm sure glad we were at the last of that line because I think Mr. Chadwick had worn down by the time he got to us. Anyhow, he told me that night I didn't get the paddling the bigger ones got, but I got enough. I thought we were going to get another one from Mama when we told her what we had done. There I was, in the third grade, and I already had a paddling from the Principal. It taught me a good lesson: I knew not to do that anymore. I have never forgotten that third grade lesson in discipline.

I don't remember much about the fourth grade. Our teacher was Mrs. Vivian Delamar and we were in one of the dressing rooms in the gym.

Mrs. Delamar and I are kin - her mother and my grandmother were sisters. She was asked one day by one of the other children if, being we were kin, did that mean I wouldn't get a paddling if I needed one? She told them that being kin didn't have anything to do with it; if I needed one, I would get it. She kept her word many times that year.

In the fifth grade, we had Mrs. Salter. I don't remember much about that year. I always had a problem with my mouth - it wanted to talk too much. It was a good year, I guess. In the sixth grade, we had Mrs. Celia Lewis. We began to be a little more unruly as the year went on. We took advantage of her at times; even her using the paddle on us didn't seem to make much difference. We got through it without a lot of problems and we all passed our grades; we felt pretty strong by then.

The seventh grade was one that I remember well. We started out with Mrs. Stella Sadler. She agreed to teach us until they could find a teacher for us. Well, in about ten days we had driven her crazy. Mrs. Adelia Ross then agreed to come in and teach us and in about two weeks she was ready to quit. By then, we thought we could run anybody out; nobody was going to push us around. But things were about to change. One morning, this big woman walked in, prepared to teach. It was the Principal's wife. She had with her a big paddle and we knew she was able to handle it. She was friendly, but very business-like. She went to laying down her rules and telling us what we were going to do and what she was prepared to do if we didn't follow the rules. For the first couple of days, things went smooth. But as the days went on, we began to test her to see how far we could go. We soon found out, for she went to using that paddle.

It wasn't long before everybody in that class had felt that paddle, sometimes two or three times a day. I always envied Barden Carawan because when she put that paddle on me, it hurt, and I would cry. Not Barden. He would lay up on that desk and she would pour it on until she got tired and he would get up looking like he hadn't felt a thing and go back to his desk. She brought us down to where we needed to be and she taught us the rest of that year. She had our attention and if she didn't, she knew how to get it. Her name was Mrs. Waters. I will never forget her. In the eighth grade we had Mrs. Ivy Jones. I remember one day when Cliff Potter brought in a big rat that had been knocked out from something they were experimenting with in a science class. He tried to give it to Mrs. Ivy, but she got on top of her desk. We learned quite a lot from her; she would use the paddle when it was needed to get our attention.

I started the ninth grade with the belief that anything I made over a passing grade was wasted effort. This was high school and we had basketball and baseball and we changed classes with different teachers. Our homeroom teacher was Mr. Tom Shelly, who had just got out of the service. The Second World War was over and the things he told us about it were very interesting. I remember he told us that he had trained to be a bomber pilot, but when he made the flight to certify him, when he landed the plane it touched the runway and made a little hop back up in the air before touching down again. They didn't like that, so they didn't certify him. Mr. Shelly said that was the best thing that ever happened to him because many times during that war, he was glad he wasn't a bomber pilot. We had a very good year with him, and we learned a lot.

In the tenth grade we had Mr. Guion as homeroom teacher. He was also the basketball coach, so we played a lot of basketball that year.

Hobucken High in 1990

There were some more bright scholars that joined us in that grade; one was called "Stakes." Curtis Ireland was his real name; he was from Lowland and we soon became best friends. Our idea was to do a lot of playing and a little studying, so we barely got by, but somehow we passed our grade.

In the eleventh grade we had Mrs. Pope as homeroom teacher and Mr. John Hamiltom as Principal and coach. I don't remember much about Mrs. Pope. I guess we learned some; Stakes and I were doing about the same in our studies. One day we were practicing basketball. We had enough players to have two teams, so we chose up sides and went to playing. We were playing pretty rough, and after a while something happened between Leamon Bateman and James Almond and the fists started to fly. They were fighting pretty good when Mr. Hamilton came in the door. He came right over and broke it up; he said he thought that by now they knew lemons and almonds didn't mix, and sent us to our rooms.

There was enough going on that I was interested some. Mr. Hamilton let me run the movie projector and I was taking French, although I told them that those crabs and fish didn't care whether I could speak French or not. I still know "je vous aime," which means, "I love you." We had good summer fishing, so I bought me a 1929 Model A Ford roadster. My studies were about last in my life, but I continued to go to school and pass my grade.

The twelfth grade was a struggle. I was interested in everything but school - my roadster... girls... fishing. My report card showed it, too. Stakes and me were seeing who could do the worst. On one report card I had two C's and two F's. When I took it home, Daddy said of the nine children in the family, it was the worst report card that had ever been in the house. I told him if he thought that was bad, he should have seen Stake's - he had all F's. But what Daddy said hit home with me, so Stakes and I started to do better. I was told I would have to go another year if I didn't pass, and I didn't want that.

I remember one incident in the twelfth grade: there were about thirty of us boys out back of the gym, smoking. We had picked up some kids in our class who had been in the military and had come back to school to finish their education, so we talked about marching. One day around school, we lined up in pairs out back and came out with Bennie Jones calling "cadence." It was during dinner and nobody was allowed in the school building unless you were sick, or some other reason. We marched around outside for a while in complete formation, with others joining us. Finally, we headed for the front door of the school building. Some teachers saw us coming and met us at the door; we paid them no mind and went right on in and marched up and down the hallway. Somebody went and told Mr. Hamilton. We were still marching when we got word he was coming, so we broke up and started looking for a way out. Fred Alcock and I headed for the front door and ran into Mr. Hamilton. He grabbed both of us and told us to go to the office, which we did. Mr. Hamilton soon came in and told us to go on to our room; that there were a lot more boys in it than just us. It wasn't long before he came around with a pad and pencil, taking names. In a little while, we were all in his office. We were given a choice: to take a paddling, or write a theme of 5000 words on how to behave in school. Almost all took the paddling.

The 1999 destruction caused by Hurricane Floyd

Our teacher's name was Mrs. Selma Van Horn Whitley. She was a good teacher and we learned a lot from her. I know now I should have studied harder. I graduated in the spring of 1950. I know it was a relief to Mama and Daddy when it finally happened. I was glad it was over, too. We had good teachers all those years. It wasn't them; it was me. Unfortunately, I didn't see the need to learn. I planned to work on the water and stay right here. I shrimped the summer the Korean War broke out and I went into the military in November. I saw very quickly that in order to get ahead in this life I needed more education, so I enrolled in all the educational courses I could take, and I'm still learning all I can.

Tar Kilns and Tar Pots

When you leave this island heading up Highway 33 towards Aurora, in a couple of miles you cross over into Beaufort County. About four hundred feet into Beaufort County at the first turn in the road, on the right, there are three, and possibly four, tar kilns. I'm told that's what they are called.

About a year ago, I was at the fish house. Some hunters told me about these doughnut-shaped pots on the side of the road, just over the county line. I soon got into my truck and went up to find them.

After much walking looking for them all over the area, I headed back for the road. That's when I found them, right next to the turn in the road. There is also a well there, about one hundred and fifty feet away from them towards the county line. I'm told that this well was dug around 1920 by a logging crew for their animals to drink out of.

I looked over the tar kilns real good, trying to figure out the layout and how they were used (the center pot still had some wood in it from the old tree).

I have found a place on Fulford Point at Lowland that is about twenty feet square; the land is about two feet higher than normal, and there's a ditch all around it leading to a well. This place is level on top, with no sign of a pot-like place in it.

I also talked with Keith Cowell, who lives at Arapahoe. He told me there was one on his property. One day, we walked back to it; it's about like the one at Fulford Point – there's no sign of a pot in the center, either. The ones at the county line are different.

There has been a lot of work done with a shovel to make these things; they fit in with what I have been told about them. They are built on rising grounds in a doughnut shape six to eight feet across, with a hole in the center. The bottom is higher than normal ground, making it easy for them to drain.

I have been back several times, looking over them and taking pictures of them. I have talked to a lot of people, including Bill Mason, about how they worked. Everybody tells me they burned wood into them and caught the residue to make tar.

I have looked on the Internet and in the library for information on them, but I haven't found much on just how they worked. I finally found an old book at an antique shop, written in about 1915. I got more from it than any other place. Here is what it says:

"Tar is a thick, black, sticky product, obtained by the destructive distillation of such substances as wood, coal, peat, and shale. Wood tar is made from pine, fir, and larch trees. Sticks of green pinewood about three to four feet long are piled up in a conical shape, and damp earth and sand are heaped over the wood to a depth of several inches (This crude stacking method is still extant in the Carolinas, Georgia, and Alabama). When everything is in readiness, the pile is ignited and allowed to burn slowly for about ten days. As the tar is melted out of the wood, it is run into retorts, where it is distilled; wood spirit and pitch oils are given off. The black residuum is poured - while hot - into barrels, where it soon hardens and becomes the ordinary tar of commerce. As much as 150 barrels of tar are taken from a single hole. This product is used for preserving timber, for caulking seams in ships, and for other industrial purposes. It is also used in medicines and in ointments and skin lotions."

There are many places in the area where these pots are said to have been, so I know that, at one time, it was big business in this area. It usually takes time to walk into the woods to find these types of pots, but the ones at Fulford Point are right alongside the road, so for anybody who wants to look at this type of thing from the past, it's just a matter of stopping and looking at them.

In looking at the location of these pots, I realized they were in an ideal spot for getting the product to boats for shipping, because of transportation back in those days. I'm sure that the road we use today is the same as it was back then, because the road from this way goes directly to the pots, then turns a little and goes on to Smith Creek. If they were shipping south, they would come this way to Jones Bay. To ship north, they would go to Smith Creek and go down the Pamlico River. It would save them a lot of time shipping like this.

In one book I read that one of the pots blew up and killed somebody, so I guess they were dangerous. I think resin is part of the process, too.

When we first started trawling in Pamlico Sound in the late forties, there were a lot of chunks of resin caught into our trawls. You could break it open and it would have the prettiest color to it; most of the time, it was put back overboard. I don't know whether they catch any today or not.

I have been in touch with John Oden of the Beaufort County Historical Society about these pots. He told me they would try to get someone to look at them to see if they had any historical value.

I'm not real sure just what they are; if they are tar pots, it doesn't look like they were ever used, there is no residue around them that I could find.

I'm sure they are manmade. They are in good shape to have been built around the turn of the century or before.

Perhaps somebody will know what they are; they are quite interesting to me.

The Road Plow

In 1946, a construction company from South Carolina started to pave the road from Cash Corner - about where the Vandemere turnoff is on 304 - to the end of the road in Hobucken.

Now, this road in Hobucken was very narrow - probably no more than 20 feet wide. Since only a few old automobiles ever used it, people had never seen anything plow the roads and ditches besides an old hand-operated machine pulled by a four-wheel drive truck, which moved very slowly. When we heard it coming, we would run out to the side of the road to watch it go by.

When this company came in it had some old dump trucks, a couple of old drag lines, and what looked like a brand new road plow like the ones we are accustomed to seeing today. To begin preparations for paving the road, one of the first things they had to do was clear the sides of the road and move the ditches to where they are now, which added approximately ten feet to each side of the road. Out in the wooded areas, where there were a lot of roots and stumps, they used the draglines to move the ditches, but here in Hobucken they used that brand new road plow hooked together with a small bulldozer (It didn't have enough power by itself to plow the new ditches as deep as they needed to be).

It just so happened that on the evening they were to move the ditches, we children were on our way home from school. They were coming down the road on the south side going east with the brand new plow and that bulldozer hooked to it. Just about everybody was standing out on the side of the road and some were standing on the road; nobody had ever seen anything like this before. Naturally, there was curiosity to see

45

where the new ditches would be and what the road would look like after they were moved.

Well, the plow had no trouble going down the south side of the road. It then turned around and started back up the road, plowing a new ditch on the north side. The plow was just wide enough for the wheels on one side to run in the old ditch with the wheels on the other side running in the new ditch it was plowing.

In front of Eugene Lupton's house, there was a little water in the old ditch. When the plow and bulldozer got to that point, the plow lost its traction, the wheels started spinning, and it began to sink down with the blade going deeper in the ground, and the bulldozer couldn't move it. It went down until its bottom was lying on the ground and its wheels were spinning.

By this time, all of us school children on our way home had gotten there and all the parents in the area were onlookers, too. Those who had children coming from school came out to see why their children hadn't come home yet, and when they saw this, they came to look. Surely, almost everyone in the eastern end of this community was looking on.

Mr. Joe Styron was running around saying, "I would tell them how to get the thing out, but they won't ask me." Almost everyone was talking about how to get it out, offering different ways.

The old plow

46

These men did have a problem because the best and strongest piece of equipment they had was stuck, and I mean STUCK!

I'm not sure just how they did finally get it out, but I think it took two dump trucks and that bulldozer to pull it out after much shoveling to help free the blade.

So now, when anything exciting happens in Hobucken, you will probably hear someone of the older generation say, "This is the most exciting thing that's happened here since the road plow got stuck."

Things that Happened During my Brother Charles's Life

EGGS

During the winter of 1962-63, Charles came from Texas to fish out of Organ Inlet for flounder and bass. (The winter before that had been quite a good season to make money.) The boat's name was *Chris F. Two.* The crew consisted of Ben Gaskill, Sr., who was the cook, Marvin Peed, the deckhand, and myself. I was in charge of the engine room. That time of the year, you have a lot of bad weather to contend with, but by watching the weather closely you can get some working days. Then you work non-stop until the weather runs you in.

We were tied up in Wanchese on account of the weather and one morning Ben had cooked breakfast and called us to eat. I was in the engine room, so I came on up. They were sitting at the table waiting for me, so rather than hold them up, I sat down so the blessing could be said and they could go to eating. Then I got up and washed my hands and came back to the table. Ben had cooked a dozen eggs and a pound of cheese. They had taken out what they wanted, I thought, which was about half of what he had cooked. I took that fry pan and dumped what was left in my plate, and went to eating it with hot biscuits.

The weather was bad, so the next morning we were still tied up to the dock. Ben called for us to come and eat breakfast, so we all went into the galley. Charles was washing his hands. When he noticed the fry pan on the stove, it was level full. Ben had cooked two-dozen eggs and two pounds of cheese; it was all eaten. He said, "There's nothing wrong with this crew if they eat all of that." Ben said, "That's right, yesterday I wanted more of those eggs, but I didn't get them. Today I'm planning to get some more." Charles said, "I saw that, too, but I didn't say anything."

I told them I thought they had taken all out they wanted the morning before and I didn't want Ben to throw the rest away.

We had a standard breakfast after that. Everybody who knows Ben knows that the language I used here was not like what he used most of the time.

A FAMILY FUNERAL

My brother Charles was a hard worker, always looking for a way to make a dollar and ways to save one, if he could. One of the ways he talked about was to have a family coffin stored at the funeral home. His plan was that when somebody in the family died, we would be taken to the funeral home in our best clothes, put in this coffin, and then be open to the public for the funeral either at the funeral home, the church, or the graveside.

After the funeral when everybody was gone, the coffin would be taken to the cemetery, where the body would be taken out and put into a cardboard box and lowered into the ground and buried. The coffin would then be taken back to the funeral home and stored until another member of the family needed it, and then this procedure would be repeated.

I don't know how many funeral homes would go along with this.

BREAKFAST WITH JOHN

We were raised up - all nine of us - with different ideas as to how we would live our lives, so we went in different directions. Some of us stayed close and some of us moved away.

In the early seventies (and a lot of years later), some who had moved away got to moving back home for their retirement years. Eunice and John sold out in New Jersey and moved to New Bern, finally moving in with Daddy at the old home place. Charles and Mary sold out in Texas - boat and all - and moved back to their home here.

John went to working on the house and was staying busy doing things for other people, as well as working in his shop. Charles went to work around his house, using a bush ax to chop paths through the woods back of the house so he could walk to the old white oak corner without being torn up by briars. He put in pipes and filled in the ditches for easy walking. He did a lot of work. He also went back into our family history.

After about five months of this, he told me that being retired was the worst job he had ever had. He just had to get him another boat and go back on the water.

He and John headed south to look for a boat; he said he was going to go to the Gulf and visit boatyards and docks where he could find a boat he wanted, even if he wound up in Texas.

One morning at about 6:30 when they were in Bayou La Batre, Ala., they decided to go to the only cafe in town for breakfast. John said it wasn't what you would call a first class restaurant, but if that was all there was there, it would have to do. It was called the Gateway Cafe, and it had a wide range of things on the menu.

There were four men sitting at a table with a pitcher of beer when Charles and John went in and sat down. A young black lady came out of the back and over to their table. They ordered bacon and eggs and hot coffee. When she brought the coffee to them, John said it looked like it

49

had been made the night before; it was so strong and only lukewarm they couldn't drink it, so they decided to wait for their meal.

They kept waiting and waiting. After about thirty minutes, John decided to go in the back to see what the holdup was. When he got back there, he couldn't find anybody. As he headed back out to the table, the back door opened and the same lady came in with some dirty eggs on her arm; he said she had chased some chickens off the nest to get them. He asked her if he could help her. She said, "Mister, I sure wish you would, because I feel so bad." She gave John the eggs and went and lay down. John fixed breakfast and served it to Charles and himself. I asked John if they had to pay. He said they did. I don't know whether they left a tip or not.

Our Status Symbols

Man has always had his status symbols - today we see people riding in Cadillacs and Lincolns and automatically we think they must be doing all right; we rate them pretty high without knowing anything about them. This is nothing new. Around the turn of the century, it was horses and mules, buggies and carts; the more you had, the better off you were. Today, there are more people who buy a new automobile every year. Some buy one every two or three years, and some run them until they fall apart. It was the same with horses and mules; some people would swap horses, quick.

There were always horse traders traveling around. I remember a sign that Mr. Ruff Alcock had hanging in his store. On it, someone had written: *Swapping hosses is all right if the other man has the best hoss.* I was told these men would swap, thinking they were getting a better animal, but it wasn't always the case.

There was a horse trader named Mr. John Hobbs who came around every week. He would be in a buggy with one horse pulling it and about four others tied to the back. His business was to trade or sell you a horse and, most of the time, he would make a deal.

Just east of where the Masonic lodge is in Bayboro there were stables where your animal would be looked after while you took care of your business. It cost fifty cents to unhook and feed a horse and put him in a stall, one dollar to keep him overnight. Most of the time, if a man had to go to Bayboro, it was to go to court or have a deed changed. It would take a horse about three hours to trot to Bayboro from Hobucken.

At the beginning of this century, just about all anyone had was horses, but by 1920, most everybody was changing to mules. They were cheaper, easier to break and manage, and a lot of other little things that made them better to work. People would keep a horse or two just for getting someplace quick.

I remember my older brother telling me about Uncle Roger Spencer using a mule and a horse hooked up together to pull a mowing machine to cut peas. Uncle Roger was sitting on the back of it. When they came out to the end of a row to turn around, the old mule laid down, so Uncle Roger unhooked him and hooked himself up alongside the horse, and continued to mow his peas until he was done. He said he didn't remember what happened to the mule.

There were a lot of horses and mules in this community at that time. Mr. Bill Williamson and Mr. Henry Williamsom had horses; Mr. Charlie Henries had a horse and mule; Mr. Amos Ireland had a mule; Mr. Carl Alcock had about a dozen mules; Mr. Earl Peed had about three mules; and Mr. John Ireland had a mule. So by mule standards, I guess my family was at the bottom because we, along with Uncle Fred, only owned Old Bill. That made us a half a mule family.

It was figured that a mule was needed for every twenty acres of land to be plowed. We had about five acres and Uncle Fred had about the same, so I guess we didn't need much of a mule. I heard Daddy tell Mr. Jim Gaskill that when his old white mule died, he wanted to get some parts off him to use as spares for Old Bill.

As far back as I can remember, we had a cart with black spoke wheels. We used it for a long time until one of the wheels went bad. The wood rotted away so they had to get another wheel. Somebody here in the community had a complete cart they weren't using, so Daddy and Uncle Fred bought it. It was a pretty cart; fairly new with red spoke wheels. And it was a little bigger than the old one, so we could haul more with it.

After we had that cart a few years, the wood on one of the wheels rotted away on it, too, so we had to pull that old cart out of the back of the stock house in order to take the two good wheels and make one that we could use. We took the wheel off the big cart and put it on the smaller cart. It worked, but now we needed a long leg and a short leg in order to stand up straight because now the cart wasn't setting level. It didn't seem to make any difference to Old Bill, but that big wheel would wobble. Daddy said he was afraid to pass anybody because the wheel would sweep them in as they went by.

I can tell you, having a cart like that wasn't all that bad; when I wanted to find Daddy and he had taken Old Bill out with it, I could tell that wheel print on our dirt road from all the rest by the wobble it made. That was the last cart we ever had. It was the end of the mule and cart days, the end of an era.

LET'S TALK HISTORY

Indian Village

When you drive down the main road in Hobucken, you come to where the pavement ends. You keep going down the dirt road until it ends in approximately three more miles. When you have to stop, you will see the Cameran Lodge, which is setting on piers about twelve feet up off the ground. The Johnson Lodge is across on the north side (not visible), and you are at the head of Middle Bay.

At the water's edge on the north side of the Cameran lot, are the remains of a shell and pottery pile that was left there by the Indians who lived there many years ago. This area was covered by scrub oaks then; it was where the headquarters of the tribe were. There is another shell pile on the north side of the creek that the Johnson Lodge is built on. Most of us think that there was a tribe on each side of this bay.

The shell piles that are at Middle Bay were reduced in size many years ago when the land in this area was broken out and farmed. The farmers needed lime for their fields, so a lot of shells were hauled out by mule and cart and put in the fields. Some were hauled up here and are in these fields. My father hauled some for Uncle Jack. There are still a few men living who can tell about it. Over the years, when the land was being farmed at Middle Bay, there were many arrowheads found in that area. I saw one when I was a boy that Mr. Roosevelt Parson caught in his oyster dredge, just down the creek from these shell piles. Sam Swindell told me he has found many arrowheads during his lifetime in this area.

There is another big pile of shells close to Jones Island on the south side of Jones Bay, down at a little creek called Little Ease. The west end of this pile was out when I was a boy.

Sam Swindell

55

There have been bones and spear points caught just off shore of it by different people in their oyster dredges. During the winter when the water gets clear, you can take a small boat and see just how big this pile is. I'm told that it is covered with silt now. (Most folks are sure there were one or more tribes of Indians over there, too.) It takes about 800 feet of net to go offshore around it when it's fished.

There are cemeteries here that are said to be Indian burial grounds. There's one at Middle Bay, over in the woods on the south side of the road. It's called the Brickyard Road Cemetery now; old folks called it Cordons Corner Cemetery. The last person was buried there in June 1913. There are about fifteen headstones there, but Sam Swindell says he can see the markings of thirty-two graves. He is sure some Indians are there, also.

Ray Hathaway

On the west end of Hobucken is a little dirt road going north called the Pole Cat Road. Ray Hathway told me that when he was a boy, his family farmed some of that land. There was an area in one field where he was told to raise the plow as he plowed it, because there were some Indians buried there. He said he never saw any bones or anything to show it. On the school-house road around behind the Edmon Jones farm (Ronnie Gray lives there now), there were some graves in the woods running north and south with stones on them. Charlie Jones, who grew up there, told me about them. The old folks ahead of him didn't know how they got there. Nobody knew. In digging a ditch across the back of their farm, they broke in the side of one of them. He said he didn't see any bones, but he did

Charlie Jones

see some wood that was in the ground. They were told it was an Indian burial ground.

Uncle Walter Hopkins told that he saw part of a human skull when he was loading some of the shells in his cart from the Middle Bay shell pile, so we know some Indians were buried in those shell piles.

Verona Swindell's grandfather, Mr. Jim Spain, lived close to those tribes at Middle Bay. Her grandmother Polly said they felt sorry for the Indians when they were told by the govern-ment they were going to be put on a reserva-tion. After all, the Indians were here first.

Sherwood Sadler

Some of us have been told that we had Indian blood in our family. I guess relations weren't always good between the white man and these Indians. Verona and Sherwood Sadler both told of a white child who was kidnapped by the Indians and taken down to Middle Bay. The men in the surrounding area waited until dark, got their smoke poles, and went down there and surrounded the village. They had the child tied to a stake in the center of the village and were dancing around it, chanting their trib-

al slogans. The men rushed in from all sides to surprise them before they could get to their weapons - which they did - and rescued the child before any harm was done to it.

The last Indians anybody saw in this area were some that came into Drum Creek by canoe. Everybody was sure they were looking for the area where the Indians had been at Middle Bay, and got in Jones Bay, instead. They stayed a few days and disappeared. Nobody

Verona Spain Swindell   knows what happened to them.

This information did not come from any history book; it came from different families. They or their folks have lived here at Hobucken at some point in their lives, and it was passed down to them from past generations. I'm not closing this; it will remain open. I will add to our history of this area as I learn more from other people who are willing to share and I'm studying the history books to find out more.

Indian shell pile

Is this the village that Captain Ralph Lane and Sir Richard Grenville observed as a Secotan Village near Hobucken in 1585? or Mr. John White's 1587 Indian village of Secotaoc? According to Mr. White's map, they were close to where the present-day town of Hobucken is. Based on the physical evidence at Middle Bay and what has been passed down through the generations to present-day folks, I'm sure they were.*

According to the Goose Creek Island history book, up to the start of this century there were thirty-two families living in that area, and some of the cisterns and chimneys are still there where their homes were. I have pictures of some of them. My grandmother grew up down there and they farmed some of that land. All of that area – as well as where are today - was called Hobucken.

---

* I read the following in a recently published book by Mr. Joe Mobley called _Pamlico County – A Brief History_: "In 1585, a second expedition to Roanoke Island (forerunner of the Lost Colony) led by Captain Ralph Lane and Sir Richard Greenville, sailed on exploration of Pamlico Sound. During this voyage, they passed the mouth of Pamlico River southward along the Eastern shore of present day Pamlico County. There, they observed Secotaoc, a secotan village, near what is now the community of Hobucken.

Interesting note: while reading the Mayo-Jones history book, I saw that in 1763, Francis Jones bought from James Ellison a plantation on the north side of Bay River at the mouth of a creek above "King Sothell's cabin at the head of Vandemere creek- 640 acres." King Sothell was king of the Bay River Indians.

How Mr. Joseph William Clayton Discovered Goose Creek Island

By Mrs. Carrie Lupton Lewis

Joseph William Clayton, known as "Joe", was born in Tyrrell County. His parents died of high fevers when he was four years old. He was raised by family members and friends, never staying in one place very long. His uncle, Henry Lewis Clayton, lived in Beaufort County and occasionally Joe would make the trip from one point to the other on his uncle's sailboat, which was called a kunner. The coast of North Carolina is not a smooth coast; it's made up of many, many peninsulas, called points.

One time, when Joe was heading home with a fair wind after one of these visits, a storm with heavy rain and wind overtook him. He had to take his sails down and steer his boat by hand with a tiller on the stern, and just drift with the wind to keep from turning over. All night, the wind blew with the rain. He was wet, cold, and tired. It took all his strength to hold the tiller against the storm. His only compass was the North Star.

When day began to break, Joe saw trees in the distance and made it to shore. He worked his boat to the westward and thought he heard voices, so he hollered, and they hollered back to him. When he reached the people, they were glad to see him; he was more glad than they were. Water was in their houses and they were hungry. Everything around them was wet and there was no way to cook. Joe had landed on a place called Jones Island.

In the past, Joe had rafted logs together to float them to the sawmills and he thought this would work now, so they made a raft out of wet logs, and using any dry limbs and sticks they could find, got a fire started. They cooked their bread in iron frying pans. The frying pans had legs on them. They found oysters, fish, and crabs, and cooked them. Joe was so impressed with seafood being right at their hand, just for the catching, and the way the people treated him. One man gave him a piece of land to build a house on and logs to build the house with, so he would stay. They thought Joe was amazing and loved the stories about his life, which had been very hard and lonely at times.

After the storm was over and the water subsided, he went to the mainland, which is now called Hobucken. He liked it even better there. Joe had a family - a wife and four children in Beaufort County - and he knew they were worrying about him and he had to go home. Bidding his new friends farewell, he set sail at the crack of dawn. Armed with his friends' advice, instructions, food, and well wishes, he headed for home. He sailed out Jones Bay, took a north course at Sow Point, then went across Middle Bay and Mouse Harbor, around Pamlico Point, and across to Oyster Creek in Pamlico River. There he crossed Pamlico River to what he called point of North Creek. It's called Ransomville today. He probably sailed about ten miles in about twenty hours. His compass going home was the North Star.

Holding the tiller on his way home, with plenty of time to think, Joe remembered a dream he once had. In the dream, he was wrestling a big rattlesnake, and by holding on as tight as he had to the tiller, he imagined he was choking it. That holding on had taken Joe to land, which turned out to be where he wanted to live for the rest of his life. He had never been satisfied and was always moving from one place to another. He felt like he had found what he had been searching for and now it was up to him to make it happen.

He probably painted a pretty picture of this new land and told his dream to his family. They agreed to move, and he came back in 1889 with his wife and four children. The children ranged in age from three to ten. One of the three daughters was my mother, Sarah Ann, and Joe was my granddaddy. He was a small-featured man with hair to his shoulders, and he had a white beard by the time I became part of his life. He couldn't read, or even sign his name, but he was a genius in many ways and had a heart of gold. I'm glad I had the privilege of spending a lot of happy times with him. He lived a good life and died at the age of ninety-four. He was buried in Hobucken, N.C., the mainland that he had discovered and loved.

I believe his dream came true with a whole lot of work and effort and sacrifice on his part, and with the help of his family and friends. But that's another story.

(This is a story written by Mrs. Carrie Lupton Lewis of Hobucken about her folks. I was at her house one day when she began to telling me about them. I asked her to put it on paper so I could include it in my book, if there ever was one. Her mother was a Clayton before marriage. I haven't changed it, so it's the way she wrote it.)

Mrs. Carrie Lupton Lewis

Goose Creek Island, July 1882
(From an old newspaper printed in Stonewall by Mr. Cahill)

With much pleasure, I endeavor to narrate names, and some of the events, of the Fourth of July picnic of 1882. The picnic was given by the people of Jones Bay on Goose Creek Island. It was, in all respects, a success. A man who was a stranger to the county could not fail to meet many friends and acquaintances. It was estimated that the crowd numbered between eight hundred and a thousand.

Among the guests were many visitors from other communities; they all seemed to enjoy the occasion to the moment. Early in the process, Mr. H.H. Dowdy of Bayboro accepted an invitation to address the people and was introduced by Mr. John Allcock. The crowd was attentive, and seemed to appreciate his remarks. Mr. Dowdy acquitted himself and was repaid with thanks, smiles, and compliments, etc. He was followed by Mr. S. Clark from New Hanover County, who entranced the audience with a brief, but pleasing, speech.

A string band was seated near a platform that had been erected for the dancers. It struck up its gallivanting songs and four or five qualities with skitrishers, polkas, etc. and was enjoyed immediately. After the dancing, the table was spread and such food as would tempt the most fastidious was placed before the most appreciative guest in the greatest abundance and variety. I have attended many picnics and enjoyed them all, but I must say - in my opinion, this surpassed all others. There was much preparation; so much zeal displaced by its managers to give enjoyment and reserve order and good feeling. No complaints were heard, and all seemed as merry as the occasion could require.

After the dinner, a heavy thunderstorm drove us all to shelter - a welcome to all at the time, as it protected us from heavy rain. After the rain, Mr. Hamlin arrived with his two daughters and several other parties. On the request of many, he consented to address the people present and was introduced by Mr. H.H. Dowdy. Mr. Hamlin made a telling speech, which seemed to make a good and lasting impression upon all his listeners.

After his remarks, we were requested to repair to the residence of Capt. Ireland, where a large room was fitted out for dancing. Here it was kept up until seven o'clock.

When our day of enjoyment was closed, friends parted and each went his way - I hope with pleasant memories of the day's enjoyment. The committee of management were Mr. Benjamin Sadler and lady, F.A. Spain Sr. and lady, Wiley Mayo and lady, Andrew Lupton and lady, G.B. Spain and lady, F.A. Spain Jr. and lady.

With many wishes for your health and prosperity.

Riggs-McCotter Cemetery at Cash Corner

One recent February, I got a call from William Howard ("Billy") and Jesse Levin ("Sonny") Riggs, who lived in Raleigh. They said that they were coming down to Pamlico County for a visit and wanted to sit down to talk a while before going back.

I went to school with Billy and Sonny in 1939; their mother was a schoolteacher here in Hobucken. With the roads in the condition they were and cars not that dependable, a person had to live close to their work. Billie and Sonny stayed almost across the road from me; we got well acquainted during that year.

Billy and Sonny Riggs

They moved on to Bayboro the next school year and lived across from the old ice plant in Bayboro while they finished up their schooling at the high school in Bayboro. I had about lost contact with them over the years.I had no idea about their Riggs name and the history associated with it in this area. But as I talked to them, I became interested in it.

They told me they would be on down, but were first going to stop at Cash Corner at an old cemetery in the woods where some of their folks were buried. I asked them some questions about this cemetery, as I had heard about it but never been to it. I asked what time they were going to be there and said that I would meet them there.

This was my thing: to go to these old villages of the past and the home sites that are there, and visit with the people who lived at these homes. I like to see the old wells and visualize what they were doing back then, and how they made a living. I like to visit abandoned cemeteries that are close by, too, and wonder about the family connections among the other people that are buried there.

Billy and Sonny and I met on the east end of the Lynches Beach Loop Road (SR 1217) between Highway 304 and Mt. Zion Baptist Church. Billy said he wasn't sure just how to get into the cemetery; he had been in it with his daddy as a boy, but didn't remember much about it other than the fact that it was as unkempt and overgrown as it is today. Billy said his interest in the cemetery went way back to a time before he went into it with his daddy because he had heard his grandfathers talking about their daddies' land near Smith Creek being bequeathed for use as a cemetery. (The land had been selected because of its elevation and access to water, as well as the land itself.)

We went to the back corner of the field and started in; it was grown up bad. Billy had some cutting pliers with him that helped some as we made our way towards the creek. Billy was ahead. After we had gone in a ways, I noticed over on our left something above ground that was made out of cement and looked like an old cistern; we headed for it. It was two above-ground burial chambers with the name William S. Riggs Sept. 26, 1852-Nov.7, 1916 on a headstone at one end of it, and his wife,

Sarah C. Riggs, May 12, 1854-Nov.13, 1923, next to it. Two children were alongside of them: Charlie L. and another unnamed Riggs.

There is a Mary H. Riggs (March 23, 1788 - Feb.21, 1858). She was a Beasley before marriage. She first married John Riggs and later married Jesse. Jesse (1781-1841) is probably buried alongside of her in an unmarked grave, with John on the other side. There are many graves marked with stones in the cemetery; we have no idea who they were, but I'm sure they were family members. The others that are marked are: William H. Riggs (1829-1885) and his wife Sarah C. (1854 –1923). William H. was the son of William S. There is Drucilla Ann Riggs (1832 –1917), wife of J.B. Flower and A.P. Barnes. Also Andrew J. Robbins (1833-1944). Margaret, wife of Samuel Riggs, lived for twenty-five years, eight months, and died in 1874. There is another set of aboveground burial chambers, but there are no names on them.

John R. McCotter (1825-1910) and his wife Sarah A. (1835-1909) are buried there. John is the son of Hezekiah and Dorcas Riggs McCotter. Dorcas was the daughter of John and Mary Riggs. Jesse and Mary Riggs had a daughter, Salina Jane, who married Eli Mayo.

There is Handy P. Hickman (1822-1901) and his wife Martha (1833-1888), and a son named

John McCotter's headstone

James L. According to Mr. Dallas Mallision's writings (he interviewed Rob Hickman, Handy's son), Handy was born in Sussex County, Delaware, and then moved to Maryland for about a year and then on to Goose Creek Island. They moved on to Vandemere about the turn of this century. Billy and his folks think that Handy's wife was probably a Robbins. (One family line from Handy goes through Sybil Hickman Forest to Forest Farm Supply at Bayboro.)

There are also some Harrises and Roses there; it looks like the last person who was buried there was Andrew Robbins in 1944. There could be some unmarked graves later than that.

The first land patent was in 1739 in Craven County by John Riggs, Sr.. The history of this Smith Creek land shows that fifty acres at the mouth of Smith Creek (which can be seen on the map) were bought from the state in 1793, and another thirty acres where the cemetery is located were bought in 1798. There were many Riggses who owned land on both sides of Bay River from Smith Creek to Tillman's Island; there are some creeks bearing the Riggs name.

In 1774, John Riggs, Sr. bequeathed to his son John, Jr. the land he now lives on on the south side of Bay River at Cabin Creek.

The first Riggses in the Mesic area were on the North side of Bear Creek. Over the years, they migrated to the south side of Bear Creek, as well as the end of Wise Neck Road, which Troy Potter told me he could remember from years ago.

Billy and Sonny's family line began in this area on the north side of Bear Creek and the Loop Road (today it's the Meekins Road) at the east end of Mesic. As with most families, their name keeps going on. In this family, it's Jesse Levin (Sonny's name); it started in 1781. They have been told that the lumber to build the house on Bear Creek was hauled from New Bern by sailboat. Billy said he saw it as a child - it was an old two-story house.

The Jesse Riggs House

Billy tells me he loved to go fishing there, and that there was another house across the road that had a raised plank way across the marsh; they walked on it to Bear Creek.

I have been told by some of the older folks in Mesic that what we call the "Old John Ives" house today is the Jesse Riggs house. It was a beautiful home in its day and it set alongside the Jim Riggs house.

Jim Riggs's house and property were purchased by one of the Mayo girls from

John Riggs' house

Mesic around 1950; the house was restored to livable condition. Later on, Mr. Peter Lozica's family purchased the property and were going to tear it down, but after looking at the material the house was built with, they decided to move it across the road and keep it. This is where it is today - it's up off the ground about four feet and I think, with a little work, could be made livable again. A lot of the people I talked to had lived in it at one time or another. Mrs. Vertie McKinney, who is 98, told me she lived in it in 1922. As the picture shows, it's a typical house of that era. All the folks I have talked to told me that those homes had been there as long as they could remember.

Hiram Mayo lives on the west side of the Intracoastal Waterway. He tells me he bought some of his land in this area from the Riggs heirs in 1968 and that they were the first deeds written on the property since the 1800's.

I went back to the cemetery several times. One day I walked on down the side of the creek toward Bay River and on the next hill down on the creek is an old home place between a field and the creek - the old trees and well are still in good shape. When you leave it heading towards the road, you see the rows where it was farmed. It was a nice place to live. As it has been with most names of this area, these families have gone west. The first Riggses were buried at this cemetery; Billy and Sonny's granddaddy is buried in Sandhills Cemetery at Reelsboro; their daddy is buried at New Bern. Three children of this family live in Raleigh, the other in LaGrange. The name Jesse Levin will end with the present Jesse Levin (Sonny). They have some children with the name Jesse, but not the complete name that started in 1781.

The Marshes Settlement

I spent a lot of time this past winter down in what the old deeds refer to as the Marshes Settlement of Hobucken. It is so peaceful and quiet there, I tried to visualize what it was like when the home sites had homes on them and big families; there must have been a lot of life there at one time. Most of the land was in cultivation; they kept all the animals they needed in order to make a living there. Joanne Spain said she picked cotton out back of where Mr. Bill Gaskill's store was. She said the stalks were tall and very big and so bushy that the sun couldn't get to the cotton bolls, so there was very little cotton to pick.

There were ditches cut from Jones Bay to some of the home sites, allowing them to keep their boats close to the house. Mr. Jim Bateman and Mr. Bill Gaskill operated stores down there; everything the folks needed to live was there.

Although all the people had moved out by the time I came along, there was one house still standing. I went with Daddy down there in the mule and cart. I feel like I'm not alone when I go down there; so much of the history of those folks is still there.

I have talked with Mr. Rufus Mason, Mr. Sam Swindell, and Ms. Joanne Spain, who all spent some part of their growing up in that settlement. They told me a lot about that area and where to look for the different things that people had on each home site. The first time, I drove down the old road that they used as far as I could to the edge of the woods, and got out and went to walking The road had grown up badly and there were trees across it from the hurricanes last summer. There was a lot of standing water, too.

I didn't see much of those first home sites. I found out later that a new road had been put in and I could drive in from

*Remains of the
Wateman Emory Sadler house*

another direction. From then on, it was a lot better.

I found old pieces of iron where Mr. Andrew Swindell operated a blacksmith shop. That area has been logged out so you can really see what it was like when it was farmland. I'm told that one of the old grind-stones is still there and I know where the other one is; it can be brought back to the community if anybody wants it.

A while back, they were having a show at the senior citizens' center. I was asked to participate in it, which I was glad to do. Before the show, I got to talk to Vera Gaskill Rice from Bayboro. She told me that her folks had lived there. Of course, I was very much interested in what she had to say. As we contin-

Brickyard Cemetery

ued to talk, she told me that she has always wanted to go down where her daddy had lived but she couldn't find anyone who would take her. I told her that she had found somebody to take her; just let me know when she wanted to go. She said she had more family members who had spoken about going down there. I told her to get everyone that wanted to go.

We continued to talk about going for about a month on the phone. We set a date to go, but it was rained out so we set another one. It was May 2nd, a Friday. When the day came, the sun was shinning brightly. It was a little cool with no mosquitoes - a perfect day for something like this. They were to meet me on Drum Creek Road where it joined the Marshes Road at about ten o'clock. I called Mrs. Nancy Winfrey of the *Pamlico News* and she joined us.

We went in the Cameron Road and drove to where Mr. Jim Gaskill's cistern was. It's a little way off the road and is badly overgrown, but it can be seen from the road if you know where to look. When I got out and started back to the other cars, I asked if they saw anything. One of the ladies already had her eye on it and was coming out. I have an old bush chopper and I went to cleaning out a path to it. That thing was so dull it wouldn't cut butter. I was moving too slow with it, so they came around me and went to the cistern and went to talking about the things that had been told to them by the old folks.

After we had been at it for a while, they said lets go to Kitt's home place, which was a little farther down the old road. As we headed for it, I saw the biggest palmetto I have ever seen right in the corner of Mr. Jim's yard and part-

Civil War headstone

ly on the road. We stopped and had our picture taken in front of it, and then we went on.

When we got to Kitt's cistern, you could tell these folks were really excited about all of it. They went to talking about what had been told to them and it was really coming out. I got out of the way and just stood there with my old bush chopper. I didn't want to say anything because they knew more about that home place than anybody else and the only way to know was to just listen to them.

I saw five generations of Gaskills there: Mr. William (Bill) Gaskill who had moved from Cedar Island with his sons (they all settled on each side of him); Kitt's daughter, Vera Gaskill Rice; Elizabeth Gaskill Cummings (daughter of Noah, who was Kitt's son); Evaglenn Clemmons from Holden's Beach (Daughter of Leonard, another son); Irma Jean Dunbar (daughter of Kitt's oldest daughter Mahalia), and Dennis Gaskill Jr., whose father was Dennis Sr., son of Noah. It had been eighty-three years since the Gaskills had moved out and now they were back for a visit. You could tell you it was very enjoyable to them. The rows where the land had been farmed were still there. On the way back to Mr. Jim's place, Irma Jean took that old bush chopper when we got to the cistern and went to cleaning the top of it off. It has a partial dome - it looked real nice after she got done with it. Right back of it was a row of cedar posts with the barbed wire still fastened to them.

Front row: Dennis Gaskill Jr. and Cap'n Dell
Back row (l to r) Evaglenn Clemmons,
Vera Gaskill, Irma Jean Dunbar,
Elizabeth Gaskill Cummings

From the time we went in until we came back out, it was two and half hours. It was one of the most enjoyable days I've ever had. The only thing wrong was that most of us got ticks.

I will be back down there next winter if my health continues to be all right and I get permission. There are some home sites that I didn't make it to this year and I surely want to go to them.

Civil War History

What I found out about the Civil War was that the federals' first line of attack in this area was to seize all the inlets and seaports along the sounds to give them control over the eastern half of the state. This area was largely under federal control. For the most part, all the farmers in this area were small farmers. There were no plantations of any size, and few slaves. There were black landowners here on the Island, who really didn't care for war, they just wanted to be left alone to farm and feed their families and live a decent live.

According to the old folks, there weren't any major battles fought in the area, but there was a lot suffering from the pillaging and destruction of people's crops, food and livestock. There was some looting in the homes by different groups, too. According to the history books, there were groups from both sides called "buffaloes" that didn't fight for either side; they just looted and took from people of the area. The Union troops got the blame as they left the area, whether they did the crimes or not. There are stories from different families where they took barrels of salted pork and other things into the fields and put them in ditches and covered them up, in order to keep from starving. One story from Mrs. Nancy Rice of Lowland is that they buried their pork and hid the horses in the woods to keep what they had. In Hyde County, homes were taken over; feather beds were taken out; they burned all the food; and stock of every kind was either taken or killed. Gristmills that were used to grind corn were also destroyed.

There has been grape shot from the Civil War found at Gales Creek, and at the Wise Home plantation, on the north side of Bay River at Wise Neck Road in Mesic (Upper Neck today), a cannonball fired from the river went completely through the house. The house was repaired, but a hole where the cannonball went through was left showing. From what I have read, this home was like the China Grove House on the north side of Neuse River close to Wilkerson's Point.

Other men from Goose Creek Island who fought in the War were:

David G. Sadler	Benjamin Hodges
Uriah Allcock	Weightman E. Sadler
William T. Emory	Noah W. Ireland
Thomas R. Lupton	Joseph C. Allcock
Frederick A. Spain	Lewis Goodwin
Jesse R. Rice	George R. Hopkins
George Leary	

Joshua Spain served with the Hyde County Rifles.
James Bateman, Co. D. 40th. Regiment,
John W. Watson Co. G 40th Regiment
Samuel G. Swindell, Co.I 40 Th. Regiment

James Potter of Goose Creek Island, Co. 19th. Regiment, was taken prisoner and kept in federal prison at Point Lookout, Maryland. He died of chronic diarrhea and was buried there in the Confederate Cemetery in February 1864.

Amos Ireland Jr. (1840-1863) died near Chancellorsville, Virginia, in May 1863 from wounds received at the Battle of Chancellorsville with the 3rd North Carolina Troops. This is from *The Reveille* on Wednesday April 21, 1866, in an article entitled Brief Mention of a few men Formally of Beaufort County who lost their lives in the Confederate Service.

A true story that has been handed down through my family about W.T. Emory Sr. (my great grandfather) and the Civil War service was that he deserted from Fort Fisher on Nov. 16, 1863, along with two other men. (They could have been Ottaway B. Emory and Joseph C. Allcock - their desertion dates are the same as W.T. Emory.) There was a baby due at home and my great grandfather needed to be home. We don't know how the deserters got to Neuse River, but a cold front had passed and it got extremely cold and was snowing and they hadn't had anything to eat. They got a small skiff and started across the river. With the wind blowing and the snow falling, their clothes began to get wet, making them even colder. Part of the way across, they saw a light on the water. Being in the condition they were in, they decided they had to have some help. Thinking this was a Confederate boat the light was on, they headed for it.

When they came alongside, they saw the men on it; they were Union soldiers, who arrested them instantly. The Union soldiers took them aboard, where they had food and it was warm, and headed for New Bern. They asked them what they knew about the Confederate movements and if they would take the oath of allegiance and join the Union forces. After some time, my great grandfather, knowing he needed to be home, told them that if they would let him come home to look about his family, and give him something to eat, and some clothes and a little money, he would do it. They promised him they would accept him, so he said the oath and joined; the other two men did not. After he got home, the word got out about his desertion, so the Confederate forces came to look for him. He had to stay in the woods during the day. One night, they came when he was in the house. He got out of the house and hid under it. It was told that they ran their swords through the cracks in the floor, but missed him.

He is buried in the Barnett Cemetery, Hobucken, N.C. and has a Union headstone.

Pvt. Joshua Lacy Spain Jr. (1829-1892), Co. B. 17th Regiment N.C. troops (1st. organization): Born in Washington County and by occupation a farmer, prior to enlisting in Beaufort County at age 32, May 28, 1861. Present and accounted for until the company was disbanded on March 26, 1862.

Indian Island

Indian Island - an island with a lot of history - is in the lower Pamlico River about ten miles from the Pamlico Sound. Many years ago, it was connected to Hickory Point on the south side of Pamlico River, according to the land deeds (that part is almost gone). Over the years, we have heard a lot of stories connected to this island. I'm told there were holes on the east end of it from where people had dug for Blackbeard's treasure.

In the will of James Campen, dated June 20, 1758 and probated in 1762, he mentions loan of land to his son Robert Campen - land known as Indian Island.

In the book <u>A Brief History of Pamlico County</u> by Joe A. Mobley, it states that there probably was an Indian village on this island in the 1587 time frame. The Tuscarora War was waged throughout most of the colony by the Indians; they used this Island as a staging area for attacks on settlers on both sides of the Pamlico River from 1705 to1710. This, according to legend, is where it got its name.

In doing my research of the land records of this Island, it seems that nobody owned it for any length of time and most of the owners didn't live here; they lived in other cities and states and had caretakers to look after it for them. It was sold by the Beaufort County Sheriff to The Atlantic and North Carolina Railroad Company in 1873; they sold it in 1876. Up until 1956, deeds showed it to be about 700 acres.

Indian Island

The family that lived on the Island during the 1913 storm was Daniel Webster (Web) Peed and Julia Flowers, his wife; they had what a normal family would have to farm with in that day: a garden, a mule, chickens, a cow, pigs, and a sow with seven little piglets. They lost all the livestock they had except for the sow and three little pigs in a storm, according to Mr. Ivory Lupton (he's 94 and doing well). During the storm, a big oak tree blew down with the root system going over with it. The top of the root system was out of the water and the mama pig managed to get three of the little pigs up in the root system and got herself up on it, too, and made it through.

There was a fairly big house; Ivory and Mr. Walter Sadler both told me they remember seeing it while working around the Island, but they never went ashore to it. They were sure it had an upstairs. About all the land on

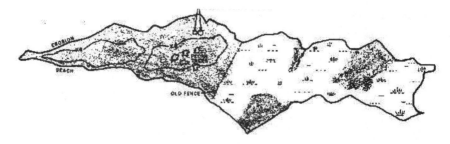

A sketch of the island in 1972

the west end was cleared; with the wind coming from the southeast, it would put the wind and waves coming from off the Pamlico Sound, going up the River and breaking on the Island, as well the other shore lines. So the wave action was coming from all directions, depositing probably three feet or more of water in the house. Mrs. Flora Lewis, a descendent of them, said she remembers hearing them say the waves were rocking the chairs in the house. The water surged over the whole Island coming in, going up the Pamlico River as well as South Creek, and the same when the water started going out; considering the situation, it's a miracle the house didn't go with it.

Ivory tells me that some men went over in a small gas boat the next morning and got them off the island; Ivory said that when Aunt Julia (that is what he called her) got out on dry land, she looked back and said, "I'm not going back. Anything I had that is over there will stay over there." They finally migrated on to Roanoke Rapids.

My father and Mr. Emory Sadler started out anchored on the South Creek side of the Island in this storm. When it was over, the boat was up South Creek in the woods. They left it when it went ashore with them and went out on Hickory Point to Mr. Jim Gurman's house, where they weathered out the storm with him and his family. This story about their experience was in the *Pamlico News* in September 28, 1983.

*Webster and
Julia Flowers Peed*

My sister Valerie went onto this Island around 1935 and said there was no house there, but you could see where one had been - the old cistern was still there and the fig bushes and pecan trees were still alive and producing; you could see the rows of where the land was once farmed.

77

One of the owners put some goats on it; people of the area would go over to it and "chase goats." Mr. Roscoe Rice of Lowland told me he had chased some years ago; he went to laughing and said, "I'll tell you, a goat can run."

Mr. Terry Cox, working around the Island over the years, has picked up two spear points; he thinks the bigger one was used to spear fish.

According to the Johnson Sisters, Veda and Opal, the last family to live on this Island was the Cannady family Texas Gulf (PCS today) purchased the island in 1967. Their deeds say there were ninety-two acres of the Island. It was leased to the Boy Scouts from 1967 to 1972.

Spear points found on the island

Mr. June Crawford, Mine Engineer with Texas Gulf, made a survey of the Island in 1972. From his report, about forty acres are marshland and the highest point was four to six feet above sea level; the remaining fifty-two acres are densely covered, and some signs of an old saw mill remain. From the slab and sawdust pile on the north side of the island, it was probably timbered out twenty years earlier. Also according to his report, there were nine large pecan trees in one group, as well as large oak trees.

I have talked to Mr. Etlas Henries, Jr. several times over the last year about going out to Indian Island. He told me to let him know when I wanted to go. On Wednesday October 18, 2000, everything came together; the weather was good, although it was a little foggy in the morning; it continued almost dinnertime.

After eating with Bill Mayo (he came along, too), we left South Creek about 1:30 and headed out. Etlas called my attention to all the old bricks on Gum Point at the mouth of South Creek that showed up after the storms last year.

When Indian Island came into view, it was a good distance from Hickory Point. As we got closer, disappointment began to overtake me. When I worked around this island in the late fifties, it was a fairly big island. Now it was small - no more than thirty acres, with big dead trees littering the shores where the storms had taken away the soil they had stood in.

The area where the house and pecan trees had been was now under water, probably four hundred feet towards Hickory Point. We went on in and got ashore on the east end of where sand and trees and marsh came together.

Etlas and I got out and began to walk back towards Hickory Point; this was where the sand and big trees were. It was grown up bad and all the dead trees lying in all directions made walking tough. I did see a stump with barbed wire still attached to it; there were some signs of ditches; Etlas said he saw another post with wire hooked to it. This was about all there was that related that man had been there. I did go onto a small beach area and pick up a few pieces of pottery; it didn't take long before we were ready to head back in.

We stopped at Gum Point where all the bricks were; they had washed all over the Point and some were still in the land. Etlas said he was told there was a grave over there. This may have been it, but it looked like there were too many bricks for that; it looked like there was a brick kiln there at one time. Just over in the edge of the woods were fairly big holes dug to get the clay to make the bricks.

I'm sure if we knew a lot more of the history of this Island there would be a lot of mysteries with it. There is still one there - about a hundred feet from the shore line on the north side of the Island is what I think is a boat rudder, made of steel, sticking bottom up out of the water about six inches, its shaft stuck into the bottom. It's in about four feet of water and it's got some marine growth on it. After Etlas scraped it a little with his knife,

79

you could see antifouling paint on it. He said he had hooked onto it with his boat, and was going to pull it up, but he couldn't move it.

It wasn't there until after the storms of 1999. Was it on the Island and with the sand washing away, fell there with the shaft going in the bottom to hold it in place as the process took place? I think there was a boat washed there during the storms, bottom up, and as it went to pieces the rudder went on down in the bottom. We felt all around it and could find nothing like a piece of a boat or anything. Etlas said he had been there with a shovel pushing it in the bottom around it, but never felt anything. So we don't know how it got there.

If somebody lost a boat in the storms they may recognize it.

Indian Tribes of this Area

In 1701, near Bear River (or Bay River today) in Vandemere, there was one town listed that was called Raudauua-quank with fifty fighting men, and another town called Pampticough with fifteen fighting men. These tribes were allies of the Tuscarora (the size of the tribes of that day was measured by the number of the fighting men they had.)

Most all of the people I have talked to at Vandemere say that where these tribes were is under water, today. I have been to Vandemere two different times, but haven't found any sign of these tribes because of the fill that has been put there to protect the waterfront.

One day, I was talking to Mr. Bud Daniels in the courthouse. He told me there were some interesting things in the library about the Indians at Vandemere from an old paper dated 1882. I immediately went there and here is what he was talking about:

THE PAMLICO ENTERPRISE, JUNE 30, 1882

"My Trip to Vandemere"

The editor left Stonewall last week for a rampage through the lower part of Pamlico County. Passing through Bayboro at 9:40 A.M., we fled away in dead interiors and reached the end of the road – Vandemere - in just fifty minutes, the distance being a good ten miles.

The very hospitable Dr. Abbot, who had the pleasure of showing us around the sawmills and gristmills especially, received us. While strolling along the beach, we were shown some of the remnants of Indian skeletons that were dug up while setting a fence post.

We brought away a packet full of these Indian relics. Quite a number of arrowheads and pieces of pottery, etc., were found. Old inhabitants say there once existed several mounds in the locality, and that frequently in cultivating the lands, whole skeletons have been plowed up.

Some parties went to the trouble to excavate one of the mounds and were successful in finding the skeletons of several human beings - all in sitting posture and in a circle.

Their bones are evidently those of the Tuscuara Indians, as history tells us that there were several of their camps in the vicinity.

I went down into the Mesic area, just up river from Mr. Tom Bland's home place; there is a lot of pottery scattered along the shoreline, but I didn't see anything that was unusual. Mr. Tom Bland told me that the pieces of pottery were big when he moved there.

Another story about Indians is from the community of Small and Walker Road of Beaufort County. While working with Dalton Walker and his brothers, Webster and Thomas, through the years, I heard them talk about all the Indian items they had found on the farm they grew up on, and a mound in a bog they believed to be an Indian burial ground, so I went and spent some time with them. They took me to a hill they farmed. Over on one side, there was a small spring of water that's still flowing today. They used it to water tobacco, so this water would be reason enough for the Indians to live around it.

They said that another brother, R. G. Walker, who lives in Louisiana, was coming home and they would call him and tell him to bring up the items they had found over the years in the fields.

On the day he was to come, I went over to Dalton Walker's home. The Rev. Rufus Walker was there, too. R.G. Walker had several items: a pipe, arrowheads, things to cut with, and a pot they had plowed up out of the ground. The pot was cracked, and he had restored it and fiber-glassed it and put a piece of plywood over the top of it, to keep it together.

Rev. Rufus Walker told me that one day when he was plowing after the time of mules had passed and tractors were being used (tractors being heavier), the ground gave way under one of the wheels, and the frame of the tractor went into the ground. He said it took a lot of work to get it out; they don't know if it was a cave or a grave that had given way. They filled the hole and continued to farm, so we will never know what made it give way.

Later on, Dalton and I went around on a dirt road close to where the Indian mound was. He was right - we had to put on our boots and wade through water and mud about a hundred feet out in a bog to get to it. There set a big mound about 150 feet across in all directions, and about twenty feet high. You get the feeling it is manmade because it sure looks out of place; it's completely surrounded by water and mud.

It's not too far on up the bog to where the water spring and Indians were, as the crow flies. There are several holes of different sizes all over this mound dug by people over the years trying to find something about the Indians, but so far, nothing has been found. There are some trees growing on it, and different people have carved their initials on them over the years. A lot of people made Sunday evening trips to set on this hill, just to pass the time. It does give you a peaceful feeling to be there on it.

The field that has been farmed over the years is full of small pieces of pottery. Rev. Rufus Walker told me that a university somewhere sent some people there years ago to look over the area. He said they used big sifters to sift the dirt, but he doesn't remember whether they found anything of value or not.

Dalton Walker sitting on an Indian mound

This is just a small part of all the Indian history; there is a lot here that probably will be never be known, but I sure enjoy digging up and writing about all of our history.

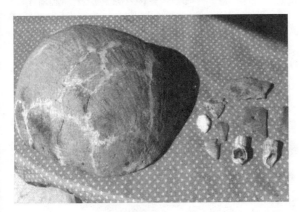

Walker pottery

Hog Island

About as long as I can remember, I have heard about Hog Island in Carteret County because my mother was an Emory before marriage and her folks were related to those of that Island. A lot of families from there moved to this Island. Since my retirement I have had the time, and the urge to go there has been greater than ever before.

When I take some of my stories to the *Pamlico News* in Oriental, I visit with Billie and Lucielle Truitt at the Old Store before I come back home. I have known them, and their folks, all my life. During one of my visits with them about a year ago, Lucille said she wanted to go to Hog Island (that's where her folks - the Styrons - came from).

Last fall, I went to the store. Lucille told me that some friends of theirs, Grady and Gail O'Neal, had taken them over to the Island in their boat. I could tell she was excited about it, as she talked about the trip and said they were planning to go back. I told her that when they went again, I wanted to go with them.

The week before Memorial Day, Lucille called me and told me to be ready to leave on Memorial Day at 6.30 A.M. from the store. Believe me, I was there at the appointed time.

When I got there, there were Dr. Dunn, his wife Mary Clyde, and their family; Ken Belanga and his wife, Sally, and their family; Ben Gaskill; Grady O'Neal, and his wife Gail; Billie and Lucille - all ready to go. We loaded up with boats in tow, and headed out.

We got down to Cedar Island about ten and launched all the boats and headed out to Hog Island. It was a beautiful day, almost slick calm. When it came into good view, the Island was full of pines and squatty oaks and a small amount of marsh on the south end. The west side was sandy with a beach. There was a camp there in about the center of it, with a good dock to tie up to.

After we got the boats tied, we went on up to the camp. The door wasn't locked, so we went in, put the boxes of food on a table, and

Hog Island seen from the dock at the camp

made ourselves at home. Most of the younger folks proceeded to get in the water to go swimming or run those little boats. Billie and myself set down on the screened-in front porch to talk, and I got my cameras out and got ready to go exploring the Island. As soon as I got my equipment ready, I headed towards the woods back of the camp and center of the Island; the further I went, the thicker the mosquitoes and yellow flies got; this area had been mowed so it wasn't bad walking.

After I had walked a few hundred feet, over on my left were some standing headstones of graves with a fence made of treated lumber around them. It was Silas Lupton (B. Aug 13,1839-D.Aug. 17,1918), his wife Joanne (B.Feb.22, 1845-D.July 8,1916), and probably their son, John Lupton (July 21,1869-D.July 20,1892), who lived 22 years, 11 months, and 29 days. Across from these graves was a wire fence with a well inside, probably to keep the animals from drinking out of it.

I didn't look much more, on account of the insects biting me, and the rest of that area was grown up bad, so I headed back for the camp.

After I got something to drink, I started walking the north beach looking for anything relating to the people. There were foundation blocks where old buildings had been - some at the edge, and some in the water. I got some Indian pottery.

I saw in the distance that there was a boat coming towards the Island in a hurry. He went to the dock and tied up. Almost every body had gone around on the east side to catch some clams. I knew he was going to chase us off, so I headed back (we hadn't said anything to anybody, we just went on over).

When I got back to the camp, he was sitting on the steps talking to Mary Clyde, who was sitting on the porch. Mary said I might want to talk to him.

He was Benny Styron from Cedar Island, a nice fella and the caretaker of the Island. I said, I'd sure like to know what you know about this Island. He went to telling me about the history of it.

Benny Styron

There were fourteen families living on the Island at one time. His daddy's name was Samuel. He operated a store over on the east side many years ago and some of his folks are buried there. Benny Styron said we couldn't go to the home place, because the insects are too bad and there were bogs we had to cross to get to it.

As we talked awhile, he got to telling me about a cemetery on the north end of the Island and a dipping vat for the people to run their cattle through. He said, "You want to go see them?" Of course, I did. We went for his boat, got in, and headed up the Island.

The soil on the north end is sandy and dry, and probably the highest in elevation on the Island, so it's a nice place for a cemetery. In keeping with this tradition, I have found other cemeteries on the highest place in other places, too.

We got to the area where the cemetery is first, so we stopped in. Benny was my kind of fella - when we got close to the shore and his motor needed picking up, Benny went right over the side around to the stern, and manually picked it up and pushed it ashore. When I got out, he came out of the water, right on in the cemetery, wearing just his socks on his feet. The cemetery is grown up bad; there are a lot of vines, briars, and scrub oaks. Didn't seem to make any difference to Benny.

There is George Emery (1820-19--) buried there, as well as some Styrons who were marked. There were a lot of headstones that had been knocked over and a lot of them were marked with just a lightwood post. Because of the growth, I don't know how many are buried there. We got some pictures of it. I got one of Benny with the Styron headstones. He said he didn't know how he was related, but he was sure he was.

We went on up to where the dipping vat is. That was a beautiful place, a lot of sand and very little undergrowth. I had a nice feeling, seeing in my mind how these things worked and the people who were there when it was being used.

Front row L-R: Ben Gaskill and Jason Dunn
Second row: Lucille Truitt, Mary Clyde Dunn, Amber Belangia, Sally Belangia.
Back Row: Gail O'Neal, Billy Truitt, Grady O'Neal, Clint Belangia, Ken Belangia,
Odell Spain. (Photo by Dr. Ernest Dunn)

We got back to the camp and everybody was ready to eat, so I joined with them. Me and Billy set on the porch. As we ate, I told him that Benny had said the area in front of the camp was full of oysters years ago - plenty of everything the folks needed to survive. We began to tell fish stories. We made some big catches there on the porch, until Billie went to sleep on me.

About two o'clock, most everybody was tired and plans were made to head back. I told them I wanted a picture of everybody before we left. I got it and we started back. Benny said they didn't keep the camp locked up, there was nothing there and they had no problems with it, so far. Every now and then in life, you have offers made to you that are too good to pass up. This was one of them. It was a most enjoyable Memorial Day.

The Beginning and End of Brant Island – A True Story

The first time I saw Brant Island was the summer my Daddy, Charlie Spain, took the job of running a boat from Brant Island to Oriental hauling fish from the pound netters who camped on Brant Island. (Brant Island was about five miles from Hobucken in Pamlico Sound.) The boat was named Edith and belonged to Mr. Else Gooding. We made a trip every day. I was about eight years old, but I remember the men who were there. I had the pleasure of meeting, for the first time, Mr. Stilly Hopkins, Mr. John Lupton, and Mr. Tom Roberts, all of who camped on Brant Island. There were more men, but I don't remember their names.

These men would get up before daylight to go to fish their nets, and return to the Island about eleven o'clock, where we were waiting in the slew for them. They would cull their fish and Daddy would hoist them aboard, ice them down, and put old sacks over them. This was all done by hand. Sometimes this was a big and hot job, depending on how many fish they had. I never went ashore on that Island that year. Haul netting was beginning to take over as a way to catch fish and Daddy and Uncle Fred had a rig, so Daddy quit and they got their rig ready and went haul netting. This was a better way as you went after the fish, rather than waiting for the fish to come to you. So I didn't go out any more that summer.

The author's father, Charlie Spain

The summers that followed, Daddy and Uncle Fred continued haul netting, and he would take me out one week during the summer. It was a trip I looked forward to each and every year. With the beginning of each year came more crews. There were crews from Lowland, Hobucken, Vandemere, Oriental, South River, and Atlantic. In the same area - and after the work was done - they all tied up to talk. I would walk a mile to be in the company of Mr. Stilly Hopkins. I wish now that I had paid more attention to these men and what they were talking about. A lot of days there was work to do on the nets and when this time came, these men would take the net skiffs and pole them ashore. There, they would pull the nets off the skiffs on the marsh and work on them. While they were working on them, I had a chance to explore the marshes and shores. Most of the fishing was done in the rivers and bays, but when the weather was good, everybody would head for Brant Island. It was further out and they could fish in the Sound and get back to the harbor pretty quickly. I was always glad when we went to the Island; it was enjoyable for me to see Mr. Stilly and the other men and go to the camps they had built there and talk with them.

THE ISLAND ITSELF

I would say that Brant Island was probably four to six acres at that time. We would always go ashore on the northwest side between the stinger shoal and the main shoal to work on our nets. (This was called

89

the slew.) Starting there and walking southwest, the first thing you came
to was the camps where Mr. Stilly and the others stayed. Their net skiffs
and powerboats would be tied in front of them. Going on south, you
came to a big cove and you had to turn back northeast to walk around it.
It was about 150 feet across. Going on south and southeast, the marsh
grass was low and the soil was dry and sandy. When you got to the southeast side, there was a small beach area and a lot of sand, which was full
of little holes scooped out by the birds. Each one had three or four eggs.
You had to be careful so you wouldn't step on them as you walked. Birds
would be flying everywhere just at arm's length from you. Going on
towards the northeast, the marsh grass got taller and the soil got blacker
and more soggy. Across the northeast-north side, the marsh grass was
taller than a man's head - probably ten feet high, in places. This side was
used for duck hunting in season. It took quite awhile to walk all the way

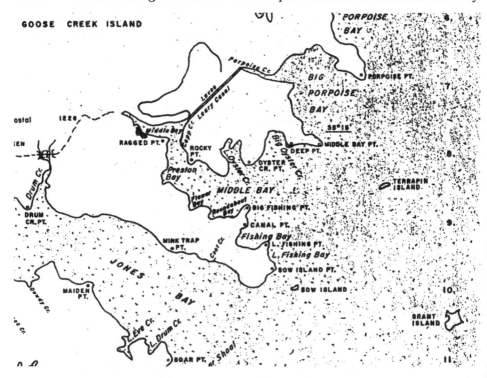

Brant Island was in the Pamlico Sound off to the right of Goose Creek Island

around it, but some days a lot of men did just to pass the time away when all the work was done on the nets and boats.

One year when I went with Daddy, we left home on Sunday evening. The weather was good and we went straight to Brant Island and anchored in the slew, fairly close ashore. We weren't there long before Mr. Stilly and the other campers came from Oriental. Mr. Stilly and John Lupton stopped by to talk to us before going on ashore. They told us that they had been told to get off the island because the military had taken it over and was going to start bombing it. They went on ashore about sundown.

THE WEEK THE BOMBS BEGAN TO FALL

On in the week, it was business as usual. We were ashore, as were other fishermen (probably thirty men on the Island), with nets pulled out, when four, four-motored planes showed up and began to circle the Island. These were propeller-driven, World War II-type bombers. They were big and very noisy. Daddy told Uncle Fred they were probably going to start bombing, and that we were going to take our nets aboard and leave the Island, which we did. We went out to the big boat - we were the only ones to leave. Everybody else continued to work on their nets.

The planes continued to circle and they seemed to establish a pattern coming in from the northwest right over us until they approached the Island. Then they finally got spaced apart, dropped down to about 400 feet, and opened their bomb doors as they came in.

On the first pass, they dropped no bombs, and they circled again. On the next run, the lead plane came in and dropped a bomb close to where Uncle Fred and his crew were working, Uncle Fred being the furthest to the north after we left.

Everybody took off running south towards the camps. When all the planes had made their runs, Uncle Fred and his crew ran back to their nets and began picking them up by the armful and throwing them into the skiff. Everybody was doing the same. Uncle Fred had a man in the bow and a man in the stern and he was in the center and they were pushing that skiff sideways, getting away from that Island before those planes had time to make another round and head back in for another run. Their target seemed to be the shore's edge.

Everybody got off the Island - except the men in the camps - and the planes continued to bomb. These bombs were falling on the north end of the Island when they started. They were not live ordnance, they appeared to be about the size of regular bombs, but they were filled with water, I suppose to give weight for better accuracy when they dropped them. They could have killed you if you were hit with one.

After they had made a few runs, it seemed as if they loosened up on their pattern and started to drop them farther to the south. They were now dropping two at a time - the bombs were flying everywhere. The men in the camps came out and got in their powerboats and left the Island, leaving their net skiffs tied in front of the camps.

Finally, one of the bombs hit the Island and went back up into the air, soaring over the top of the camps and coming down through the bottom of Mr. Tom Roberts's net skiff, sinking it instantly. Mr. Tom began to talk to those planes. He told them what he wanted to happen to them, where he wanted them to go, and that he wanted them there before sundown. He was a very upset man, but there wasn't anything anyone could do until the planes left. After about another hour, they did. Then a group of men went ashore and got overboard around Mr. Tom's skiff, turned it over and patched it, so he could bail it out and pull it on the shore to fix. He got it fixed before dark that same evening.

The events that happened that day changed a way of life that had gone on for generations. I don't know what day of the year this happened, but it's a day I will never forget.

I was on that Island every year after that, and each time there were more holes in it and the camps had been hit and there were holes in them, too.

The last time I was on the Island was in 1950 - it looked like a honeycomb: holes everywhere and they were using live ammunition, which made bigger holes.

I had to join the military in 1950. The Korean War had started, and when I came back in 1954, it was all gone - nothing but some of the stakes that had been part of the camps was standing. I felt very sad. I saw where man in about fifteen years had destroyed what had been there for centuries, and would have been used a lot more years in one way or another. But when I think back about it, had it not been bombed it would have been very small or all gone today, just through the natural process of erosion and other ways.

I wrote this because it is a part of the history of this area. I'm not against the military or anything else; it's a true story as best as I can remember and I hope everybody who reads this will enjoy a small bit of our past. I could not keep this out of my mind. All the years I worked, it stayed with me, and about 1980 I wrote it all down on a legal pad. About 1990, the school was having an auction of old school computers. I went and got some of them and ordered me a book on how the use them. Then I went to work on putting this story into it.

After I had done that - got it together like I wanted - I had no idea what I was going to do with it. After I retired in 1993, I decided to send it to the *Pamlico News,* to see if anybody wanted to read it. Mrs. Nancy Winfrey called me in a few days and told me they loved the story - to keep writing everything I knew about this area, they would publish it, and I have.

Mr. Stilly Hopkins and Mr. Emory Sadler lived down where the pavement ends here in Hobucken. There was a lot of visiting between families going on. Daddy said he heard Mr. Stilly tell Mr. Emory he didn't want to be buried close to him because all Mr. Emory wanted to talk about was fishing, and he got tired of hearing it. I guess it worked out okay. Mr. Emory is twenty-five miles away in Reelsboro and Mr. Stilly is here at Barnett Cemetery in Hobucken.

in the ground and headed for it. After I got to it, I saw the stones. One was where it went down many years ago - one side was higher than the other. The top stone had been moved about ten feet from the other one. The pry poles were still under it, so I knew that someone had tried to move it, but gave up. I didn't measure them, but I believe they were about four feet across, and that the top stone was at least six inches thick. The bottom stone was at least eight or ten inches thick.

I looked around for some of the mill's foundation. Mr. Rufus Mason (B.1906) told me that as a boy he saw some of it still there, but I didn't find any.

My daddy (B.1888) told us children that it was in operation when he was a boy and that they used wood shafts and gears in it. I thought that was all they could afford; the wood was cheap and available. I'm sure Daddy could have told me a lot more, but I wasn't interested while he was still here.

For about two years, I talked to everybody who I thought could tell me anything about this mill. I read what was written about it in the Goose Creek history book, and I got a lot of bits and pieces about windmills while working on other stories at the library.

I did learn, pretty quickly, that the wooden shaft and gears were not unusual - they were standard, and used in all of the mills everywhere. These gears had to be fairly big, so they would be strong. The arms or blades are called wings.

One day, I was in the company of Gladys Sadler (now Holton). She told me she had a picture of this old mill that was given to her by Mrs. Sina Lupton Caravan (B.1885), and that she would give me a copy of it. This came about at our Island Homecoming this year, 1998.

Mrs. Sina was Uncle Jack Lupton's daughter. She and her husband, Warren Caravan, operated a store here in the thirties and forties across from the Methodist Church. Carrie Lewis lives there now.

When I saw this picture, and the landscape around it, it just amazed me. It looks like the land was being farmed all the way from the main road (304) to Jones Bay. I believe the trees in the picture are on Jones Island. There is not a tree close to the mill; it's open land all around.

The picture shows everything fairly well at the lower levels, but doesn't show much up towards the top. The wing on the bottom can be seen clearly; the right wing shows up enough to see the lines of it. There are a few faint lines of the top wing, but very little of the left wing. I believe that some, or all, of the millhouse is there, or the wings and gearboxes and shafts would have been on the ground. It was probably a good picture at the time it was taken.

Mr. Walter Sadler (B. 1905) told me it was grown up at the mill site when he was a boy, and that the stones were there, one on the other. Everybody I have talked to about this has told me that there were trees between where the field ended and the marsh started. By the time I came along, a lot of the land was still being farmed, but the area around the mill was all woods.

I have a deed dated 1825 that states Noah Gaskill gave - out of love and affection - one hundred acres to his sister; Margaret. She had married Amos Ireland. The mill was on this property.

One of the boundaries mentioned in the deed says it's about one hundred feet from the old mill. Today, this boundary is the main drainage ditch that crosses highway 304 and runs to the fields still being farmed. It's known as the Ireland field, and Margaret was buried in it. Amos probably is, too.

According to the Goose Creek Island history book, Mr. Alfred Mayo was told by his mother, Mary Thomas, that the Yankees destroyed this mill during the Civil War and that it was rebuilt when the men got back. The history book also says that a group of men rebuilt it between 1890 and 1895. This is the mill my father remembered and told us about. According to what I have been told, Roberson Ireland bought the other men out and was the last man to operate it. The mill in the picture might not be the last one, because the list of materials and how it was to be constructed are in the Goose Creek Island history book.

According to the history book, the foundation was to be made of brick. Two sills twenty feet long and twenty inches square were to be laid in a cross (X). A hole twelve inches in diameter was to be cut where they crossed. A log 36 inches in diameter was to be used as an upright spindle; one end was cut to fit the twelve-inch hole. Twenty-five poles were to be used as braces in order to keep it upright.

The millhouse was an eight-by-eight foot square room built on two sills, which were crossed at the top of the spindle. About twenty-five steps were needed to go to the millhouse from the ground.

Four, eight-by-five foot "wings" were made of canvas and placed on the wooden frames. They were made so they could be reefed down in case there was too much wind. There is a picture in the Goose Creek Island history book by Mr. Ricky Manker of what it would look like, drawn to these measurements. The mill wing was about 60 feet to the top of it.

One of the old grindstones

From what I have found in books at the library, this is called a post mill. The Dutch name was standermolen. It's the oldest type of mill. The entire millhouse set on a spindle and was turned to face the wind by a tail pole that went out the back.

Another version of this type of mill was called the wipmolen. They look the same, but were not as high. The millhouse was round and had a domed roof, usually covered with thatch. I believe this photo may be of this type because when the photo's enlarged, you can see faint lines showing the dome.

All the pictures of windmills that I have seen show the wings in the same place. I thought they probably made a better picture in that position, but it's not that way at all. Before newspapers (or any other form of communication), these wings and the way they were set were used to tell a story to the surrounding area.

The messages sent out were: Using the twelve o'clock position on a clock face with the top blade straight up, meant to rest a short time. Ten minutes after the hour meant rest for a long time. When the wings were set about five minutes after the hour, it meant "celebration". Set about five minutes before the hour was mourning. The wings on this old mill are set for celebration.

When we look at these grand old windmills, we seem to think they are trouble-free, that they just set there and turn. But the books say it takes two men to operate it - one to look after the grinding if it's a grist-mill, the other to keep watch on the wind and the shafts and gears. The ideal wind speed makes the ends of the wings travel at about thirty miles an hour. The men love to hear them turning; there's a lot of clanking and squeaking going on. There was never any milling on Sunday; at midnight Saturday it was stopped until midnight Sunday.

I have been told there is another set of stones at the mill site. I didn't look for any more, because I didn't know it. According to history, over the years there were several mills owned and operated by different men. There is a grindstone from the Marcus Caravan mill on the side of Horn Road in Lowland that has flowers growing out of the center. It's now used for a property line marker. There are a lot of these old stones around in the different communities. Mr. Earl Ireland of Alliance told me that he was told they came from France.

The Dutch people had nine thousand of these mills at one time; about one hundred have been restored, according to what I have read.

The land we live on in this area matches the landscape of Holland. The books say that in order for the mill to work right, it needs to be on raised land and the land needs to be low and flat in order to get a good flow of uninterrupted wind to the wings. This mill had all of that; it fits the landscape.

Can't you just imagine what this land looked like 150 years ago, with these windmills dotting the landscape from the Neuse River along the sounds to Chesapeake Bay? With not much flowing water, it had to be the wind that turned them.

The inland people had streams with flowing water coming down them that they partially blocked up to make a waterfall. They could channel the water to a waterwheel to turn their mills.

There is still a deeded, twelve-foot right-of-way from the road to the mill site that is owned by Nelson Lee of Hobucken.

Note:

Stephen Jones left the pry poles under the stone. He told me he was going to bring it out to the road for people to look at, but gave up after moving it about ten feet.

Tillman's Island

Coming down Highway 304 from Mesic, heading towards Hobucken, you will see a sign on the right that reads "Jones Island Hunting Club." We refer to it as that today and consider it one big island, but it's not that way; it's actually three different islands separated by ditches and marsh, with some high land on each one.

The northwest and upper north side were called Point of Swamp or Bay House lands; the southeast end towards Pamlico Sound is Jones Island; the upper south side on Bay River was called Tillman's Island. There are places on all three where homes were, years ago. At the place called Bay House or Bay Hammock, some of the foundation blocks are still in place and some pieces of the old house planks are still there. The cistern has already gone to pieces in Jones Bay. There is a persimmon tree back of where the house used to be; when I was over there last fall, it was hanging full of persimmons.

The map shows a canal going from Ditch Creek to Gales Creek. My father told me that the old folks told him the canal was dug by the Indians. It was there as far back as anybody can remember. (It seems reasonable to me, because it would have saved them a lot of time to go from the tribe at Vandemere to the one at Middle Bay.) It wasn't too deep; there was one place where the road crossed it where people took off their shoes and waded across, and mules and carts crossed. When people going through the ditch in their boats came to the shallow place, they would get out and pull it over if the tide was low, then get back in and go on.

On Jones Island there are still cisterns where people lived. Children used to come across Jones Bay by boat to go to school (I have no idea how many).

I heard Mr. Sam Williamson say that there was a race between the boats coming across every day. He said he couldn't settle for second place, he had to win. Occasionally, he would blow the mast out or break it off in order to be first.

What this story is about is Tillman's Island and the home place that is there that's gradually going into the water as the shoreline washes away. When we went into the Marshes Settlement this past spring, Vera Gaskill Rice told me about her mother being raised up there in the early years of her life. She said she would like to go to that old home place sometime. I kept that in mind because I wanted to go, too. We kept talking about going during the summer, but the mosquitoes were too bad. I mentioned it to Hiram Mayo, who lives across the Intracoastal Waterway from this home site, and he said he would take us; that I should let him know when we wanted to go.

November 11th was a beautiful day: not cold, without a cloud in the sky, and almost slick calm. I knew the frost had taken care of the mosquitoes, so it was time to go. I called Vera that morning; she wasn't busy and said she was ready. She was going to call her cousin Elizabeth and ask if she wanted to go, too. I called Hiram to see if he was home. He was, and he said he could go anytime that day. We set out at one o'clock.

The home place we were going to was that of Sarful Emery, a name that is "colorful" according to the North Carolina Historical Review. Folks in this area have talked about this name and how he got it, for years. Some think he was named Josiah, pronounced Jo-Sar-Sar, and it varied on down to Sarful, but no one knows for sure.

Sarful, from what I have been told, was one of the bigger farmers of the area from 1860 to1885. He farmed a lot of land and had over a hundred head of cattle at one time. Vera said she heard her family talk about all the cattle pins he had when she was little.

Vera said she went over there in about 1925. Her mother wanted to go back to see if she could recognize anything of the old home place. Her folks wouldn't let her go to where the home was, so Vera stayed on the little beach there and played. She said you couldn't see the home place from where she was - it was too far in - but it's not that way today.

101

When we were going over there from the Intracoastal Waterway, you could see the oak trees where the home place was. They're leaning over towards the water now, because the water is washing away the root system and undermining them. There's also a big circle of old rocks about half-overboard. We think it's the base of the chimney of the house, but it could be from something else.

We went ashore close to one of those oak trees. It was a beautiful place for a home. The soil was sandy with no undergrowth, just big pine trees all around. We walked all over where the house used to be and found the well not too far from the house. Hiram noticed a dead cedar tree that had blown over. It had forks

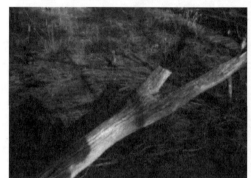

Hog killing fork

about six feet above the ground. One side of the fork had been cut off with an ax about twelve inches out. Hiram said he was sure they used the forks of this tree to put the end of a pole on to hang the hogs when there was a hog killing.

After we had looked over the home place, we started walking to the northwest. We saw rows where it had been farmed. We were looking for the cemetery where Sarful was buried about the year 1887.

We had walked awhile; you could see a difference in the land ahead of us. There were no trees in about a thirty-foot square place and a lot of driftwood was piled up all over the area. We went to digging around through the driftwood, looking for some kind of markers of graves. Over on one side, a corner was clear of driftwood and the stones of two graves were marked.

We don't know which one was Sarful's grave; they were side-by-side and adults, according to the length. We took pictures with Vera standing where she believed Sarful's grave was. You get a very peaceful feeling at times like this. We are sure there are other graves there, but we didn't see any because of the driftwood.

After we looked over the area for a while, we headed on back towards the old home place and the boat. When we got to the pile of stones at the river shore, we stopped and made some pictures of them. There were two, almost entirely white stones about the size of footballs in the pile; Vera said she wanted to take them home with her. Elizabeth asked where they came from and Vera said from the White Cliffs of Dover. We loaded them on the boat for her as

Odell Spain with friends in the Tillman Island Cemetery

we left the home place to head back to Hiram's. She told me later, that after she gets the one she has washed off good (she gave the other one to Elizabeth), she's going to put it in the house. (Roy Watson was over there fishing earlier in the summer; he has a white stone from this pile at his home.)

We were over there for about two hours. It was most enjoyable to visit there and try to picture life as it was in those days in our minds.

In a few years, all of the home place will be lost to the Bay River. The storms of 1996 did a lot of damage there. It's sandy soil and washes away easily. A few more years later, the cemetery will be gone, too. It's about one hundred feet from the water now. It is sad to think about this process; man hasn't figured out yet how to stop it. He may slow it down for a while, but eventually it takes over and goes on, and that's the way it is intended to be.

When we came back to Hiram's home, we asked him what we owed him. He said nothing; he had enjoyed going over there. As we were saying our thanks and good-byes, Hiram asked us if we wanted some fish to eat that he and his wife Pat had caught the week before. Of course, we all said yes. Hiram went into the house and brought out cleaned and filleted speckle trout and gave each of us a bag. Going over there was like eating cake, but when you get hospitality like this, it's like he put a little icing on the cake. And my friend, you can't beat that.

Some Surnames of the Area

During this past year, the *Pamlico News* expanded into Hyde County. I believe this is a good thing. Several reasons come to mind: first, the land of Hyde County matches a lot of the land of Pamlico County east of Highway 306 and Oriental North. The way of life there, the people, and the way they make a living, are all about the same as they are here.

The last three years, I have spent a lot of time in the courthouse at Swan Quarter researching my own family name. Just about all the old names I came across there are here, as well. A high percentage of the old surnames here were in Hyde County first.

When you look at the history of our country and the migration pattern of the people to this area, you have to start in Virginia, at Jamestown. The people started there and came south. They came to the Albemarle Sound with county names like Perquimens, Pasquotank and Currituck. Then they crossed the Sound and came on south with the county names of Bath, Tyrell, Hyde, and later on, Beaufort.

It is fairly easy to follow names on the old census records using the Internet. If the time frame matches up, and you look up other records, you'll find that most of the time it is the same person, and you can follow their route south. From the pattern changes in this area, it seems that after they got here, the people started going west, rather than further on south.

The name of Waitman Emery was in King and Queen County, Virginia in 1720, and in Hyde County from 1745 to 1753. According to land deeds, Mr. Emery bought land from John Squires, King of the Arromuskeet Indians. He sold 100 acres to Cason Brinson Sr. of Newse River in Craven County between 1749 and 1750. He was listed in Beaufort County as a taxpayer on this Island in 1755. The Emery name that is in both of those counties today (as well as Carteret and Craven Counties) could be from him.

Jeremy Alcock was in the Jamestown settlement. He is listed as a nineteen-year old ensign and was called a "Gentleman," according to the records. He was shot and killed three months after coming to Virginia. This is the first unsolved case in this nation. During the restoration of Jamestown, they found a skeleton that was believed to be Jeremy's. The Preservation of Virginia Antiquities is circulating a photo of a restored face, both here and in England, hoping somebody will recognize it. They can tell he was a man of class by the way he was buried. They found the shot that killed him but, as yet, nobody knows why he was shot.

There were other Alcocks who came over to Virginia. John Alcock was in King William County in 1704, and there was a Dorothy Allcock in King and Queen County. The Alcock name came from Tryell County to this area in the early 1800's and there were many Alcock families here up to about 1920. Many descendents with this name have moved away and changed the name in different ways.

The man I descend from was born in Surry County (Sussex today), Virginia, on April 30, 1753. His father was named Drury; his mother was Mildred Oliver. They moved to Pitt County in 1762. They had four sons. I descend from the oldest, Frederick Augustus, who went by the name of Augustine. The others were Thomas, Epps, and William. They all fought in the Revolution; Augustin served his time of three years and got out. When the British seized Charleston, the militia was activated to stop their move north into North Carolina. Augustine was Captain of the second North Carolina regiment.

105

After the war, he got four land grants totaling about 900 acres in Hyde County. The first was in 1783, then 1784, and 1785. They were at Northwest Creek at the head of Juniper Bay. He moved there and was living on the property of Parker Lacy, which he later bought. He was involved in the County government, taking the oath in the February term of 1785 to be J.P. He had the label of "Esquire" after his name. In the August term of 1785, he returned a list of Taxables for the lower Currituck District. He stayed in that position until 1787, when he resigned. He was back in Pitt County in the 1790 census. Christopher Mason was appointed to take his place and bought the home place. He was not a farmer; he had a business and did some land surveying in Beaufort and Hyde Counties. The last item we have on him, he was called to New Bern concerning Josiah Jones's will in 1810. He died in the Mesic area the same year.

Augustine's oldest son, also named Frederick Augustus, bought land in Hyde County between 1806 and 1808, and was there in the 1810 census. His land adjoined Foster Jarvis's land on the side of Swan Quarter Bay. He bought land on this island in 1813 and was here in the 1820 census. He had five males and three females in his family, and died 1828 in Craven County on Meekins Road, east end of Mesic.

In the 1830 census, all of his children, his wife, two of his brothers, and a sister were there. My great-grandfather's sister, Christina, married Dempsey Lupton from Hyde County. They lived in the Marshes Settlement until about 1855, then moved back to Hyde County in the Sladesville area and raised their family there.

I'm told by family members that Rev. Green Carawan started Baptist churches in three different counties - Hyde, Carteret, and Beaufort. The Primitive Baptist was started by him at Lowland in 1823. He lived up Middle Prong at the end where the pavement ends on the left side. His will was probated in 1832 in Beaufort County. In it, they were to sell the land in Hyde County near the turnpike and on Double Ditch Creek, so he was probably living here when he died. His son, Richard, got the house and plantation at Lowland. Richard sold it to Malchi Potter in 1861. There are many descendants of this man in Hyde County, here, and other parts of the country.

Rueban Slade Esq. was one of the justices in Hyde County in the 1785 terms of court. There were many Slades in Hyde County in this time frame; later on the name shows up in the Campbell and Duram Creek area, as well as this one. I haven't checked it, but the Slades in the Florence-Stonewall area are probably descendants of these people. John Sadler is shown in Hyde County as a landholder in the 1700's, along with others. They moved to this Island in the Marshes Settlement close to the head of Middle Bay. There are many descendents of this man and some of them still live in Hyde County.

The Linton name was first in Hyde County, and later here. Luke Linton got a lot of land grants in both counties and lived here on the Lowland Road at one time. There are some Lintons buried in the Barnett Cemetery here who were probably connected to these folks.

Aaron Spring was on the Elizabeth River in Virginia. He shows up both in Hyde County and here. His will is dated 1818 and the descriptions of the land he gave to his children make it sound like it was around Springs Creek; it's probably where Springs Creek got its name.

The name of Jones Bay is shown as the Great Bay on old land patten records until Frances Jones got a patten of 400 acres at the head of Drum Creek, along with other pattens. He got some in Hyde County, as well as Craven County. Vandemere Creek is known as Bandimoor Creek in 1780 on one of the pattens.

Here are just a few names that I will mention: the Gibbs and Spencer names tie back to the Englehard area; Bateman, Sadler, Cahoon, Williamson, O'Neal, Watson, Hodges, Swindell ... there are many, many more.

If all the histories of all the families from both sides of the River were put together, it would be a big book. I wish I was a younger man and had the time; it is most enjoyable to dig into these old historical records about our past.

This is just a little history of the area and a way of relating to the folks across the river. I visit and talk to some of them all the time. I'm always looking for good stories from our past.

My grandfather (1833-1895) was the third Frederick Augustus in our family line. There were three more after him with the same name; the Stonewall, and some of Washington, Spains came from this name.

This name stopped with my Uncle Fred in 1985. He and the other three are all buried in the Barnett Cemetery here at Hobucken. As for the first two, I don't know where they were buried.

Hobucken Drawbridge

Gateway to Goose Creek Island, N. C.

Hobucken Bridge at the Intracoastal Waterway has affected many people's lives. Some are mad when they have to wait for it to close, and some don't care - they just take it as a part of life and go on, not worrying about it. But I can tell you, it has come a long way from what it was when it was built in 1929.

It was one of the most modern bridges built in that day - one man could do it all. The fact that it was not a fixed bridge, but a bridge that you could swing open, made it unique. People would come just to watch it being opened and would get on it and help crank it open.

In those days, freight boats and a sailboat that was used to make a living with, were about all there was to open it for. There were very few pleasure boats, so it wasn't opened all that often. But a man had to be there around the clock to open it when a boat needed to go through.

It took awhile to get the bridge right to open. The bridge tender had to walk to the east end gate and swing it around to close it, and then to the west end gate and swing it around to close it. Then he had to go back to the center and take a big steel crank down which stood on its end against the side of the bridge, and drop the big square end through a hole to unlock it. The handle extended over to where it just missed the side of the bridge as you went around with it; that took two complete turns. What was going on was that the wedges that are under each end were being pulled out.

Then you picked up the entire crank and moved it to another hole about three feet away and dropped it in. This was where you had to be a good man, because it took every ounce of push you could come up with to break it loose to start it moving and to keep it going. Sometimes if the wind was blowing, it would stop you, and you would hold until you could go again.

I have talked to some of the men who cranked it open many times and they don't know how many times they went around in that twenty foot circle in order to open it all the way, but I know it was a lot.

Top view of Hobucken Bridge

Most of the time, those bridge tenders were glad to get all the help they could when it had to be opened. During weekends, we boys would help. Even if we were swimming, when we heard a boat blow, we would run to get on and help crank it open. You can bet it was kept greased good, so it would crank as easily as possible. But even with all that, it took a good man.

There have been a lot of things that happened at the bridge there since it was built. I guess the first mishap was in 1935. One of the bridge tenders opened it and forgot to close the gates. It was during the night, and Mr. Roland Styron came up and didn't know it was opened and ran his car into the canal. He pushed the window out with his feet and got out before the car sank, but the waterway was blocked until his car could be lifted out.

During the Second World War, Victor John Brignoli, who now lives in North Brunswick, New Jersey, was a Marine stationed at Cherry Point. He married Norma Carawan from here on Saturday night, and on Monday morning, he had overslept, he said, so he was running a little late. When he got to the bridge, he realized too late it was open, and busted through the East gate, ruining it and going on up to the edge. By the time the car got there, it was moving enough to roll over and the front bumper caught onto the fender pilings below and stopped, standing on its end. Victor was afraid to even take a deep breath. He couldn't take his foot off the brake, because the slightest movement could have made it go on in the water. He set still until they got some ropes tied around the car, and made it fast to the bridge.

They had opened the bridge to let a menhaden boat go through. The Captain saw the situation and knew they couldn't close the bridge with that car on the bridge locks, so he stopped his boat. He had a free derrick where a boat usually hangs, and he put it over the car. They hooked the cables on the car and they lifted it back up on the roadway. I guess everybody got out of this all right. If that had been another type of boat going through, road traffic could have been tied up for many days.

During the war, there were Army men stationed on the bridge around the clock. They changed the guard around six a.m. One very cold morning, four men in a transport carrier were on their way to change the guard. It had sleeted during the night and everything was covered in ice. You could fall down just trying to walk, it was so slippery.

On this end of the long straight stretch, coming from Mesic, the curve is elevated quite a lot. (It was dirt at the time.) When they got to it and started around it, that truck lost traction and skidded sideways, right on down until it went in that canal and lay on its side with about four inches out of the ice and water. Three of them got out immediately. It was dark, and they realized there was one who had not, so they went back and found him and got him out. One man headed out walking towards the bridge to get some help; the other men were trying to keep that last man awake. He was almost drowned and they were all about to freeze.

Mr. Charlie Ives was on watch at the bridge. He called Jack Carawan, who lived close, and his own family, too. Jack and Charlie went on up there to help get the rest of those men to the bridge house. Charlie's wife, Ms. Mary, and his daughter, Gladys, came over with hot coffee and blankets for them. These men were so cold when they got to the bridge house they had a problem keeping that last man out of the truck from wanting to go to sleep. They knew if he went to sleep he wouldn't wake up, so they kept pouring the coffee in him and wrapped warm blankets around him, and making him walk around some to get his body temperature up. They all survived. I guess this incident was the closest to a death associated with the bridge, so far.

The first improvements were made in about 1948; they installed a set of levers and shafts and made the gates so they would lift up when pulled. It took a good man to pull them. You can bet they were kept greased good, but it was better than having to walk to each end - they

111

were on the south side at center. A little later, they added the house you see now on the north side, and put a little engine and transmission in it, and made it so this would open the bridge. The old crank was kept in case it was needed. I was in that room awhile back. It is all done by a computer now - a few switches, buttons, lights, and electric motors.

According to the records at the bridge, the most boats and openings in one month was in October 1987 when 3,030 boats went through and it was opened 1,168 times. The total for the year was 18,648 boats. It was opened 9,675 times in 1988; 18,915 boats went through, but there were only 7,964 openings. I guess 1988 was when they went to opening it twice an hour. The most boats going through in one opening was during the Second World War, when 92 P.T. boats went through. It took between three and four hours for all of them to pass through. You can see this is a very busy waterway, and it hasn't been without its own set of problems.

Here are a few:

When this waterway was constructed, mostly freight boats used it. Their length was from 150 to 200 feet. They were built of very heavy material, were very wide, and carried about a twelve-foot draft. These boats ran in the ocean along the coast before this waterway was built.

In early 1941, the freight boats *Eastern Shore* and the *City of Salisbury* met just south of the bridge. As they attempted to pass one another, the *City of Salisbury* caught a shear from getting too close to the bank and it put her out of control. Going north, it headed towards the center set of fender pilings. Having the tide going with it, and being loaded, it was so heavy there was no way to stop it. It hit the fender pilings, knocking them down, and went right on into the end of the bridge before stopping. Then the tide carried the stern around until it went against the bank, blocking every thing up.

My older brother, Thomas Spain, was on watch on the *Eastern Shore.* When this happened, he stopped the boat and let the tide carry it on back to the *City of Salisbury,* where they got a line to the stern and pulled it back around out of the pilings. Nobody was hurt, but there was a lot of damage done to the fender piling system.

During the war, there was a lot of damage done to the sides of this waterway by those P.T. boats. Those boats made big waves and the men ran them at full throttle. When the local fishermen saw them coming, they would leave the docks with their boats to avoid having them washed onto the docks. According to the Goose Creek Island history book, on January 12, 1943 at 10:00 A.M., one of these P.T. boats stopped at the Coast Guard station. The young man in charge was sick with the flu and needed a doctor. The station commander called Dr. John Bonner from Aurora. He came to the station and treated him - his name was John F. Kennedy. We know a lot more about him now.

All the years of operating this bridge, the pedestal it sits on has never been hit by water traffic; the fender piling system has had its share of knocks. The underwater power line has been cut several times, but there has never been a major accident to stop its operations more than a few hours at the time. If an accident happens and it looks like it will take a while to repair it, they go get a tractor and hook ropes to each end of it, one to pull it open and the other to close it. The road portion has been worked on a few times. The guardrails on each end have been beat-up on the most. As I write this, the rail on the west end is all bent up where somebody has been into it. They have been changed several times over the years that I know of.

For those of us who choose to live on this Island, this bridge is a part of our lives. We deal with it every day, and most of us don't mind waiting for it to close. It gives us time to slow down and look at what is going on around us; a chance to talk to our neighbors while we wait; to see the beautiful boats that go through and the barges and tugboats as they pass. Sometimes, we walk up and talk to the people passing through.

This story is about history, about the things that have been done to the bridge during the years it has been in operation. In a few years, it will be replaced by a high-rise bridge and it, too, will become history. I will be one of the first to say it's time for it to go, but it is a landmark for our area, which I hope won't be forgotten.

I want to thank all the people who helped me get this together. Some of this information came from the Goose Creek Island history book, which is available. I learned a lot myself - things I heard about over the years, but knew very little about it until now. I encourage all young people to take pictures of it so future generations can see how it was in our day.

On Sunday, Dec 10, 1995 at about eleven A.M., Gene Potter was killed under the east end of this bridge. Pie Sawyer was having a problem getting it to open, so he called Gene, who came and went under it to fix it. Gene told him by radio to open it. In doing so, Gene was crushed. I don't think they know what happened. He died in just a few minutes, as I understand it.

Hobucken Methodist Church History

At the time the Methodist Church was organized at Hobucken, there was no church building. The preachers that came to the community held services in a building called the Alliance Hall.

The Alliance Hall belonged to an organization known as the Alliance Order. This building stood on the land where the present day Methodist Church stands, and served as a community building for elementary school, church, and civic affairs.

In 1895, Rev. John C. Jones came to Pamlico County and was sent to Hobucken and Lowland to preach, conduct funerals, visit the sick, and perform all the duties of a preacher. He held services in the Alliance Hall each Friday evening. On October 6, 1895, Miss Joella Mayo (Sadler) became one of the first members of the Methodist Church. By 1901, there were six on the roll. They were: William T. Emory, Sarah J. Emory, Richard T. Parson, Annie Parson and Marcus B. Sawyer.

These members began to talk about building a church building. Marcus Sawyer pledged one hundred days of free labor. People who owned timber pledged trees and free labor - they cut and hauled timber to Frank Spain's saw mill on Doll's Creek Road, then hand-planed the lumber after it was sawed.

William T. Emory and his son, Charlie, Richard T. Parson and his son, Will Murf, sawed the cypress trees at the commissary at Springs Creek. Ellis H. Pickles of Bayboro gave forty dollars to purchase the land for the church site from Rufus Alcock, which was up Doll's Creek Road just to the South of the Pentecostal Church parsonage, about a third of the way to Doll's Creek Landing.

The Board of Church Extension gave three hundred dollars when the building was started and one hundred dollars for three years after that, until the building was completed enough to worship in. This was approximately 1911.

From roughly 1906 to 1910, Rev. Frank Fulcher from Ocracoke, NC, held several revivals, and many of the local people joined the church. By 1910, there were thirty-six on the church roll.

The people really began to work on the new church - giving money, as they were able, and donating free labor as carpenters, etc. William T. Emory acted as supervisor of the work and when the steeple was finally added, it was a Negro who did this; he stayed at Mr. Emory's home during his work. Emory and Foy Sadler painted the church the first time. William T. Emory and Josiah Hopkins were the first church trustees.

Over the years, the superintendents were: William T. Emory, Augustus Sadler, Pelage Goodwin, Mrs. Joella Sadler, Fred Spain, Mrs. Charlie R. Spain (Annie), Ellis Gaskill and Hiram Lewis.

The first wedding in the church was Arnold G. Sadler to Martha J. Parson on April 5, 1924, with the Rev. William C. Jones officiating. Pelege Goodwin and Charlie R. Spain were witnesses.

Roads were being built, and the Methodist Conference asked that all churches be moved to state-maintained roads. Mr. Charlie R. Spain and Mrs. Joella M. Sadler were present when the relocation was ordered. Land had to be found to move the church onto and as the present site was in the center of the community, it seemed to be ideal. Mr. and Mrs. Denard Sadler (Joella) bought the Alliance Hall and moved it, and traded the present land for the Doll's Creek Church land.

Methodist Church in 1910

These deeds are in two parts: 1928 and 1931. The trustees at this time were W. T. Emory, J. W. Robinson, and Wm. Murf Parsons. The Methodist Conference helped finance the moving of the church to its present site in approximately 1928. Mr. Lodge Credle, a respectable black man from Mesic, was hired to move it.

In 1933, the church was blown off the blocks during a hurricane. Mr. Johnnie Spain was in charge of re-blocking it; he and other members of the community put the present blocks there to help.

In the 1940's, the side steps were added to the vestibule, replacing the front entrance steps. Four classrooms were also added.

In approximately 1952, the church was removed from the Stonewall charge (which included Stonewall, Bayboro, Alliance, and Vandemere) to the Aurora charge, with Campbell's Creek and Warren's Chapel. Warren's Chapel was moved to another charge in the 1960's, so there are only three churches in the charge at the present time. The pulpit furniture was purchased in the early 1950's by the W.S.C.S.

The Fellowship Room was added in 1958, taking in one of the classrooms.

The church was originally heated by a wood heater, later with a coal heater and, finally, gas heaters were installed in all the rooms. An attic fan and other small fans were used to cool in summer.

In 1963, a new hardwood floor was put down and white asbestos shingles were put on the outside.

In 1969, the central air and heating system was installed, with all duct-work put in under the church.

In 1972, the inside paneling and restrooms were completed. In the same collection, the land from the west side of the church to Doll's Creek Road was purchased from Denard Sadler's heirs for a parking lot. The money was raised by pledges taken up by Mr. Bert Robinson. Pledges were made for new pews and chair seats for the sanctuary. In March of 1973, the pews and the present carpeting were installed. About this time, vinyl siding was put on the outside of the building.

Kirby Spencer and Mr. Lienster Spain were the adult class teachers for over 20 years. Kirby Spencer has been the carpenter for all the work on the Church for 15 or 20 years.

The W.S.C.S. members and local people of the community have done a wonderful job of raising funds and contributing their time to keep the Church in good repair and also make needed improvements. Each fall there is a bazaar and dinner for the purpose of raising money.

Today, there are 124 on the Sunday school roll and 91 on the church membership roll. Church member Mr. Kirby Spencer is the lay leader of the charge, which includes Aurora and Campbell's Creek.

The present teachers for Sunday school are:

Mr. Odell Spain	*Adult class*
Mrs. Birma Alcock	*Young adult*
Mrs. Reba Lupton	*Primary*
Mrs. Rita Lupton	*Kindergarten*
Miss Irma Lewis	*Intermediate*

117

The Secretary and Treasurer of the Church are Mrs. Royce Spain and Mr. Bert Robinson.

Many names of faithful and dedicated people have been left out of this Church history due to a lack of records. It would be nice to be able to mention each and every one that has had a part in the building.

1999 was a bad year for our church building - termites got into the foundation sills and floor beams. All the under-structure of the vestibule had to be replaced, as well as the walls up to eight feet.

Over the years, we have had three hurricanes: Dennis, striking twice; and Floyd. Because of them, there was water in the church, which did much damage to the hardwood floors. Almost half of them had to be taken up; some were replaced, and some were repaired and put back down. After the building dried out, all of the carpeting had to be replaced. We had all the ductwork replaced, too, and put overhead.

We had a lot of help from the Methodist churches all over the country; some people came from as far away as Farmville to help us get the carpeting out and clean up.

Floyd came about a week later. There was more water in the church and then there was a tornado, which came from the southeast, traveled almost parallel with the main road, and crossed the road about Lover's Lane. It did much damage to home roofs, and took the Will Murf Parsons home off the blocks and destroyed it. Most of the outbuildings of Uncle Jack Lupton's were completely destroyed, and some of the Methodist church roof was taken off as the tornado passed just across the road from it. It went on across an open field, hit the Pentecostal Church and the old school building on the Loop Road, and destroyed both of them.

We never lost but one Sunday service through it all, Thank the Lord.

On August 6, 2000, we had Mr. Marsh and wife visiting us from the Youngstown, Ohio, Methodist Church, where Mr. Marsh is the Pastor. This church helped us during the past year in our time of need - they gave us new Bibles that are in the church today

May 2000: Not much has changed from 1970-2000 in our membership, except it has gone down over the years. There are about fifty on the roll today. Church and Sunday school attendance goes from fifteen to thirty each week. More people are moving out of the community, so as an older member passes away, there is no one to take their place.

August 27, 2000: The contractor finished up. It's been a year since the water came into the church. We have had all the outside sills replaced and some of the floor beams from about the first pew to the back of the church. Some electrical work has also been done. A lot of money has

Methodist Church in 2000

been spent on things that had to be done in order to lift the church higher to keep the water out from future storms.

Most of the money came from the Duke Foundation and other Methodist organizations through the country. They have been a lot of help to us in our time of need. Our thanks to the Lord and the others that gave.

May God bless us all.

(I have included this story because it's part of my entire life and my children's early life. My mother's father, W.T. Emory, helped build the church and was involved with it all of the years he lived here. My mother became superintendent in the 1940's, and is credited with bringing the church membership up to levels never known before. She was in this position until the 1960's, when she asked her son-in-law Ellis Gaskill to take the job. He did, and it remained in my family until about 1978. All of my family up to the present day has made this church a part of their life. We had a lot of help from many good community people, making it a big part of the community.)

Saving the Hobucken Post Office

In August of 1994, we received a notice that our post office in Hobucken was to be closed. The lease had run out on the existing office and there was no other building available; everything was in place for this to happen. When our school closed in 1968, about six of us had gotten together and incorporated so we could get the residence the principal was living in deeded to the community. We thought we could use it for a community center. Later on, we got the school building also. We told the people in the Charlotte post office that we had this building available and would do what was necessary to put the Hobucken post office into it. Then we went to work to try and get the existing lease extended to the first of the year, which we did.

We had a meeting of interested people and decided what we would do; it was going to take quite a lot of money and work. I was asked by Mr. Roy Watson and Mr. Carl Alcock, Jr. if I would take the job of getting the work done, using volunteer workers. I told them that if they had the money, I had the time.

Our plans were approved by the Charlotte office. We went to work on Nov. 21st tearing out the walls, the wiring, all the kitchen appliances, one bathroom, all the sheetrock, the front entrance, and the existing outside siding. We boarded up all the windows, too.

Some days we had up to twenty people working out there, from all over the area. Chief Dan Lamont from the Coast Guard station came down along with his crew. Things were moving along well.

About Dec. 20th, the Greensboro office (which had jurisdiction over the Charlotte office) rejected our plans and told us that they were not going to extend the lease on the old office. We went back to the Charlotte office and got the lease extended until July 31,1995. That gave us time to look at what still had to be done; we were about seventy per cent complete. We worked on until the middle of January and finally stopped. I had serious doubts about doing any more.

We were sent a new set of plans and had to hire an architectural firm to see if we could make the new plans work without undoing a lot of the work we had already done. We couldn't. We stayed on hold, and continued to talk to the people in Greensboro.

One day, two young men from the postal department showed up to look over the building. James Cavanaugh and I met them there. We were in complete frustration about where we were headed. We had put in all of the walls about where we thought they wanted them to be.

Old Hobucken Post Office

James was a good worker, working every day. He was very good about taking things out and keeping the floor clean, and could hand you things that you needed to work with. He understood the problem very well.

As these men talked among themselves, one said to the other, if we change the window, then a beam has to be taken out. (Mr. Hubert Potter had put it in and finished it up.) When James heard him say that, before I could even think, he had already made a statement. In very sharp, clear, understandable English, he told them "H— no, G.D., if we are going to take that out." I grabbed him by the shoulder and told him not to say anything else; let them do the talking, which he did.

About the middle of April, we got a phone call from Greensboro telling us that they had scrapped those new plans and that we could go back to the original plans, but we had to make some changes.

We started back to work the last week of April and worked six-day weeks until August 3rd. There wasn't as much help as there had been last winter - everybody was working on the water. There were only two of us that worked everyday during this period, but we got it so they could move in by the deadline. There were only a few loose ends that needed to be tied up.

New Hobucken Post Office

James and I worked on this project for 143 days, along with a lot of other people from the area. It was an uphill battle all the way. I guess I enjoyed it - we now have a first class Post Office, which I am proud to say I helped keep, for now.

I couldn't mention all those who worked in this story, but I had to include James. Even though he was handicapped, he worked very hard and every day. The beam is still in place; I guess they listened to him.

One more thing: I don't want any more volunteer work for now from anybody.

YOU HAVE TO LAUGH

Uncle Jack's Coffin

Among the old folks here at Hobucken and Oriental, I don't believe there is any other name that starts people smiling as quickly as this name when it is mentioned. He was Jack Lupton, better known as Uncle Jack to everybody in this community. He lived almost in front of the Methodist Church and his home was a gathering place when there was a problem in the community, such as the 1913 storm or some other disaster. He was a very likable person. His testimony in church was, "Don't do like Jack does, but do like Jack tells you to do." He loved to tease and play pranks on young folks. Just about everybody I talked to told me a different story about Uncle Jack.

Uncle Jack's property was laid out so that his fenced-in area for the mules and cows ran parallel with the road, and his barn and workbench were not far from the road. He would be out alongside the road, which was dirt at that time, and when he saw the children on their way home from school he would throw a penny in the dirt and watch the kids plow around, looking for it. Or he would say, "I'll give you a nickel if you will eat that fly right there," and point to one he had just killed. One time when the children were on their way home, he had braided the hair on the tail of his mule and had ribbons tied to it. Everybody told me about this next paragraph.

The good book tells us to be ready to die, and we all know we're going to one day. But few prepare for it like Uncle Jack did. With the help of his grandson, James Carawan, he built a coffin for himself to be buried in when he died. It was not just a square box, but one that was tailored to fit his body. The end for the head was a little bigger than the end for the feet, with the widest place at the shoulders. It was painted black inside and out. He had a cotton lining made for the inside, with a row of tacks with bright heads to go around the top; he was to be put in this at the time of his death. He took it into the house to store it under his bed so it would be handy when he needed it, but Aunt Emmaline wouldn't let him keep it there. So he took it out and stored it up in the rafters of his barn.

After that, when he saw some children on the road, he would take it out and lay it where they could see it and get inside of it. He would wait until they got close, then throw the top open and raise up and holler, and watch them scatter. Or he would try to get some of them to lie in it, just to see if they would fit. I don't think he had any takers, but he had a lot of fun with it.

Mrs. Linkey Parson told me she helped him throw corn in the barn one year and he told her to be very careful not to hit his coffin; that he was going to be buried in it and he didn't want it damaged in any way. There were other men who said they worked with Uncle Jack and were familiar with that coffin.

When Aunt Emmaline passed away, he remarried and moved to Oriental, but he was not forgotten by the people here. I understand he did

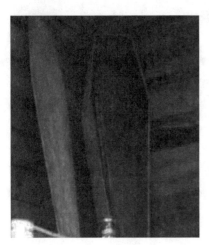

The coffin at rest

some remarkable things there; one time he stopped a robbery that was in progress at a store. I don't know much about it, but I'm sure if you ask some of the old folks who have lived in Oriental all their lives, they could tell you about it.

Uncle Jack is buried at Oriental; I was at his grave a few weeks ago. I am told that he wasn't buried in that coffin, but nobody knows what happened to it.

Uncle Jack. Gone, but not forgotten.

Mr. John Wilson and the Snake

As far back as I can remember, the men who lived in this area and farmed the land here also worked on the water to help make a living for their families. They would put their crops out in the spring, and then go fishing or crabbing until cold weather, when they harvested the crops that had grown all summer. Even if they were only farmers, most of them had a small boat at the creek so they could go catch a mess of fish when it worked out for them.

Over at South Creek, there is a small creek called Muddy Creek that goes up by the docks on into the woods. It's a good place to catch fish using a cane pole, but the cottonmouth moccasins were bad up there; you had to be on the lookout all the time. (During mating season, they would puff up and get sassy and come right at you to attack you.) The best way was for two people to go - one could look out for the moccasins while the other fished.

Libby Brousard, who now lives at Aurora, grew up there. She told me that she and her sister were fishing up that creek one day when one of those snakes came at them. Her sister hit at it and missed, so she hit it again and it coiled up right around her fishing pole. She gave him that pole and left the area.

Mr. John Wilson was a farmer who lived in the area. He had about thirty-five acres of land, and was considered a fairly big farmer for 1940. He was busy most of the time, but sometimes it would work out that he could take his fourteen-foot skiff and go catch some fish.

One time he wanted to go fishing up Muddy Creek. He knew the snakes there were bad, so he took his gun with him for protection. He paddled on up there and got on the bow and started fishing; the fish were biting real good so his mind was on fishing.

After he had fished a while, he heard a thud in the back of his boat. When he turned around, he saw that a moccasin had come over the side of his boat and was in the boat with him. He grabbed his gun, quickly loaded it, took aim at that snake, and pulled the trigger. He killed the snake, but now he had another problem: his boat was sinking because he had shot a hole through the bottom of it. He grabbed his paddle and went heading for the shore as fast as he could. He made it before it sank.

He pulled the boat partly out and found some old rags which he stuffed in the hole. By paddling a little, and bailing a little, he got it back to the dock. Nobody knows whether he took any fish home or not, or what happened to the skiff.

Bill Mayo tells me that the snakes are just as bad today up that creek as they were when this happened.

An Unusual Coon Story

In the days when everybody used cotton webbing, all mullet fishing was done at night. The fish could see the webbing in the daytime, and you couldn't catch any. There were several men here that mullet fished all the time. One of these was Sam Swindell. Sam was fishing one summer night in 1970, down Jones's Bay over on the Jones Island side, close to the mouth. It was about midnight; he had put his net out with each end of it as close to the shore as he could get it. After it had set awhile, he decided it was time to fish it, so he turned a light on, took a pole, and pushed his skiff to the end of the net, putting his boat against the bank.

He put on his rain suit to keep from getting wet, and was just starting to fish his net, when a raccoon jumped out of the marsh and clamped onto Sam's leg and thigh. He didn't make any attempt to bite him, he was just holding on. Sam dropped his net, took both hands, and grabbed him by the back of the neck, and threw that coon back in the marsh. The coon jumped right back and clamped on his leg again.

Sam got his pole and pushed the skiff away from the bank a little and threw him back ashore, so he now couldn't get back the boat. Sam said he knew how to deal with him because he had a baby coon when he was a boy. It would lie in his lap just like a cat, but Sam had to get rid of him when he got big, because he got mean.

That night, the coon followed right along on the shore as Sam fished his net. He threw some fatbacks and pinfish on the shore for the coon to eat, but he didn't want them. When Sam got to the other end of his net (that put him back close to shore), that coon came back aboard. This time, he went in the fish Sam had just taken out of his net, and got a trout. Sam grabbed him, the fish and all, and threw him on the bank. He threw a couple more fish out there and rushed the skiff off so the coon couldn't get back on, and left the area.

Different people saw this coon along the shore over the next couple of days as they passed in their boats. About the third day, Marcus Gaskill, his brother Eddie, and James Bateman, was out on the sound side of Jones Island with what you call a swiping rig. This type of fishing you have about a half-mile of. You put one end ashore and head off shore with the other end, using a power boat; swipe it around, taking in as much area as you can; and bring that end back around until both ends are together. You use the power boat as much as you can, but when the pond gets small, you have to anchor it and everybody gets overboard and pulls the nets by hand to finish up. This is called "footing."

They were doing this with Eddie closest to the shore, in about four feet of water. They needed a pole and there was one on the bank, so Eddie went and got it. As he turned and headed back to the net (about four feet from the bank), that coon came running out of the marsh and jumped on his back, attacking him. Eddie lost his balance - the coon was biting him on the back of his neck through his raincoat. Eddie was under water and couldn't get up and the blood was running. Eddie said later he thought the coon was going to drown him. James was the closest, and started for him, but in that depth of water, you can't move too fast. James was a big and strong man in the arms and shoulders. He was in good health and when

131

he got to Eddie, he hit that coon with his fist just as hard as he could on the side of its head, knocking it back on the bank. It shook a little, but didn't get up. James had knocked him out. James got Eddie back on his feet; he was bit pretty badly on the back of his neck and across his shoulders.

They started working as fast as they could to get the nets up, so they could bring Eddie in to go to the doctor. After a while, that coon came to and headed into the marsh. Nobody saw him after that.

Sam believes that somebody had him as a pet and as he got grown, he got mean, and they put him on that island to get rid of him. Eddie had to have stitches on some of those bites, and was mighty stiff and sore in the neck and arms for two or three weeks, but he got all right.

I don't believe you hear much about man being attack by a raccoon, but that's what happens here.

A coon in back of Vernon Swindell's house

Mr. Kelly Ross and the Bear

Before crab pots came along, people used a baited line to catch crabs with. It was called a trotline. It was about a mile long, and the bait was spaced about every four feet from one end to the other.

The bait was pickled and was called "bull nose." Actually, it was the ears, tongue, and other parts of beef that couldn't be used for anything else. All of it was cut into small pieces and kept on the boat in a special container so the flies couldn't get to it.

Each man had his own kind of buoy to go on each end. It didn't have his name, or any number on it, like they do today, but if a man came upon another man's buoy, he could tell whose it was and what way the line ran from it, just by the way it was made, or the color of it.

These men went out before daylight to get what was called "a set". The idea of this was that the crabs would come up on the shoals and along the shore at night, and when they started back off to deep water at daylight, they would cross this baited line, and the men could catch them in their dipper as they went up and down.

About 1950, Mr. Kelly Ross of Lowland had a twenty-eight foot boat he used for crabbing. It had a cabin on it and a V-8 flat head Ford in it, which would cut off if he opened it up too quick.

One morning, he left the dock at Oyster Creek just before daybreak, and headed for the Pamlico River to find him a set. The moon was shining bright, so you could see fairly well. On towards the river, he saw what he thought was somebody's crab line buoy, so he headed over to see whose it was. He steered his boat so he would be close to it, and he slowed down his engine so he could get a good look at it.

By the time he realized it wasn't a crab line buoy, but a fairly big bear that was swimming, the bear already had lifted up one of his paws and had hold of the side of his boat, and was going along with him.

Mr. Ross reached over and opened the engine throttle all the way, just knowing it was going to cut off. But it didn't, it took it. The force of the water against that bear didn't make him turn lose - the bear reached up with the other paw and got a better hold. He went to bringing up his back paws and started to digging on the side of the boat. When he got a toe-hold after much digging, he came up the side and came in the boat, not far from Mr. Kelly.

Mr. Kelly decided it was time to move, so he ran forward and got in the cabin, closed the doors, and stood there with the top hatch open so he could keep an eye on that bear. The engine was running wide open, the boat was going around and around, and the bear was checking his crab barrels.

Mr. Kelly said if that bear had come up to the cabin, he would have just let the boat go until it cut off, or ran out of gas, or some other reason. He wasn't about to come out and challenge him. The bear crawled all over the barrels in the stern and then went overboard on the opposite side of the boat that he came aboard on. Mr. Kelly was sure relieved.

Mr. Kelly came on back to the dock. He was so upset he didn't put out his line that day. It probably was too late when he got clear of that bear.

Wherever that boat is, the scratch marks that bear made when he came aboard are still on the side of it.

Mr. Jim Spain's Joke with the Sawyers

James Spain, who was called Jim, was a brick mason by trade. He built a lot of the chimneys and cisterns in the homes of this area, as well as the foundations of some of the churches and other buildings. All of the men in his family line were of this trade. Brick masons of Hobucken were John G. Sadler, Simeon Sadler, James P. Spain, and his son Johnny C. Spain.

James P. Spain (1862-1931) learned his trade as a brick mason from his Uncle Henry in Kinston, NC. (Note: all the males of the David Spain line were brick masons: James, his son Johnnie here at Hobucken, Henry at Kinston, and Jerome at New Bern.) Brick masons jobs were building cisterns, laying foundation blocks for homes, and building brick homes. The brickyard was located on Brickyard Road (now Cameron Road) and is said to have been in operation during the Civil War and up to the year 1900.

James P. Spain

134

Mr. Jim's Joke

By Lola Spain Caraway

(This was taken from the Goose Creek Island History book.)

James Spain, who was known as an old man as Jim, liked to play tricks on people and enjoyed a good joke. This is about one he played on Mr. Bonner Sawyer and his wife Nellie, who lived in the Marshes Settlement southeast of Hobucken. They wanted a new fireplace and chimney, so they asked Mr. Jim if he would build one for them the following Wednesday. Mr. Jim studied for a minute and then told them, "You don't want it built next Wednesday. If you build it on a growing moon, the smoke will not draw through it." Mrs. Nellie, although a superstitious person, said she didn't believe it; she wanted the work done on Wednesday. Mr. Jim said, "Okay," and warned them again that they would be sorry.

Bright and early on Wednesday, Mr. Jim commenced to run the chimney. We don't know whether he completed the job that day or not, but when it was done, he fastened a piece of paper across the top of the chimney. Then he hollered to Nellie, "I'm finished. Go build your fire, but you'll see the smoke won't draw through it."

Mrs. Nellie quickly built a fire and soon the house began to fill with smoke. She and Mr. Bonner didn't know what to do next; after all, Jim had warned them and they hadn't listened.

All the while, Mr. Jim was standing around looking smug, and secretly enjoying his prank. Finally, the Sawyers asked, "Jim, isn't there something that can be done?" Mr. Jim suggested they could tear it down and wait until the moon changed. Of course, that didn't appeal to them. After a bit of thinking on this matter, Mr. Jim said, "I don't know of but one more thing. I know this little verse. I can go on top of the house, wave my hand across the top of it, and say the verse. Then I believe the smoke will come through it okay."

Naturally, the Sawyers were skeptical, but at this point they were willing to try anything, so they went ahead and told him to do it. Mr. Jim climbed up on the roof of the house. As he recited the verse, he began tearing off the paper from across the top of the chimney. Smoke began to pour out of it.

Mr. Bonner and Mrs. Nellie were delighted. They were very grateful to Mr. Jim for solving the problem and really happy with the new fireplace and brick chimney.

Mr. Jim got a big kick from the joke he played on them and told it many times. We never heard whether Mr. Bonner and Mrs. Nellie found out the truth.

Mr. Robert Hopkins and his Cork

It used to be some years ago, that when a man wanted to go somewhere in his skiff he either poled it or sailed it - probably some of both. But as times changed, engines became a reality and those who could afford one adapted their boats to use them pretty quickly. These engines didn't have a lot of horsepower and they vibrated badly. If a boat wasn't in good shape, it would shake so bad, it would make it leak to where a man had to stay with it all the time to keep it from sinking. The only way these engines could be used by most was to run them slowly to keep everything together.

Somebody came up with the idea that if you took a net cork and trimmed the outside of it down to where it would just fit into the horn of the carburetor, and let the engine pull the air through the center hole, it would run better and cheaper. It wouldn't shake as badly, either, so everybody had to have one.

One time, Mr. Robert and Mr. Jim Gaskill were oystering in a bay that was closed for some reason. Mr. Robert was on the west side and Mr. Jim was on the east side when the lawman showed up. He came right up to Mr. Robert and stopped him. Mr. Jim saw him, so he took off heading for a point to go around. The lawman saw what he was going to do so he told Mr. Robert to stay right there; he was going to go get that man. Mr. Robert said that Mr. Jim had that old engine turned up so high you could see the smoke coming from it.

Mr. Robert said he thought the lawman was going to chase Mr. Jim and forget about him, so he started up his engine and had it running right slow, heading in the opposite direction. When Mr. Jim went around the point and the lawman couldn't see him any more, he looked around and saw Mr. Robert moving, so he turned around and headed back for him. Mr. Robert opened that old engine wide open and it started to messing up; he began to work on it to see if he could get it to go any faster. When he took that cork out it would do better, so he kept it out but he didn't have any place to put it. He knew he couldn't lay it down because the wind would blow it overboard and the boat was shaking so badly it might go into the bilge, so he stuck it in his mouth to hold on to it.

It was him and the lawman. He kept working on that engine to make it go faster and cutting all the corners he knew to outrun him. After a while, he felt small bits of stuff in his mouth and realized he had chewed up his cork in getting away. The lawman finally gave up the chase. Mr. Robert said he never did know his name, but that he had to make another cork for his engine so he would be like the rest.

Susie

This is a dog story. Probably a lot of dog lovers aren't going to like it, but it did happen on Goose Creek Island about 1952. It's about a female dog named Susie.

A family that moved out of Lowland left this dog to run loose in the community. I guess they figured somebody would take it in and look after it. It finally adopted Jewel Mercer and his family. Jewel had a bunch of hunting dogs in a pen out back of his house, so I'm sure it felt right at home. A lot of people saw this dog and everybody now knew it belonged to Jewel.

At certain times of the year, having a dog like this can be a problem, so Jewel told his boys Benjamin and Robbie J. to load Susie up and take her far enough away from home that she couldn't find her way back. They loaded her up and took her almost to Cambell's Creek and dumped her out in the swamp. Then they turned around. As they looked in their rearview mirror, they saw her running behind them, heading back toward Hobucken.

Susie came on back to the bridge and in a few days, crossed over and came down into the Hobucken community and had a litter of puppies under the Will Dave Ireland house. (This was alongside the Luther Gaskill house and across the road from Carl Alcock and Roy Watson's home.) There were plenty of puppies for everybody.

After the puppies got big enough to look after themselves, Luther and Carl decided that they didn't want any more puppies. The male dogs had begun to hang around after her again. They knew whose dog it was, so they decided to take her back home.

One night just after sundown, they got Susie and put her in a trailer designed to haul dogs and went up and down the road here in Hobucken. Every dog that came out, they put in the trailer with Susie until they had about fifteen dogs in that dog box. Carl's daddy had a dog that used just three legs to get around on; they loaded him up. Luther's own dog was loaded up, too.

Not being familiar with Jewel's home site, they decided to ask Roy Watson from Lowland (Jewel was his uncle) to help them take Susie home. He agreed. They went just inside Lowland to the first road and turned right going to the Primitive Baptist Church lot. There, Roy got Susie out of the box and put her with them inside the jeep they were driving, and then headed on down almost to Jewel's house. Roy took her out and walked her on down to Jewel's house to tie her down in his yard close to his penned-up hounds.

He didn't quite get her tied down when he saw Robbie J. (he was about ten years old) looking out the window, so he turned her loose. He said Susie was home, so he knew she wasn't going anywhere, and headed back.

When he got back to the jeep and trailer, they turned the other dogs out. All of them were barking by this time, and the dogs from the Lowland community were coming. They all headed into Jewel's place; his hounds were barking, too.

Jewel was sitting in his house and heard his hunting dogs barking, so he went out to find out what was wrong. His yard was full of dogs - all of them barking. Roy said he didn't think Jewel saw Susie. He knew he had a yard full of dogs, but didn't know why. He went back into the house. After they had gone to bed, the dogs got to barking so bad he jumped up and grabbed his gun out of the closet, opened the window, and said he was going to shoot some of them. (That's not quite how he said it.) But Mrs. Joella, his wife, told Jewel not to shoot any of those dogs. Two or three times, Jewel said he was going to shoot them because of their barking.

Meade Williamson lived across the road from Jewel. The next morning, he was over here at the fish house on the dock, leaning over the top of one of the pilings with his arms folded under his head. Somebody asked him if he was sick. He said, no, that he was sleepy; something had happened over there around Jewel's place last night. It was the most dogs barking he had ever heard. He said that his dog was outside barking as hard as he could, so he went out and got a hold of him and put in his pump house. He still barked and howled all night; it was a bad night for everybody.

The next morning when Jewel saw Susie, he knew right quick what had happened. When he came over to the fish house, Hugh Braddy, who was working with him, told him to go in the store and tell Roy that Jewel had killed a bunch of dogs last night. Roy told him that he knew Uncle Jewel and that he hadn't killed any dogs.

Luther told me it was about three days before his dog finally got back home, and then he just lay around a lot for a few days. All the dogs got back to their homes safe. I think Jewel kept some of them for a few days – the ones he knew who they belonged to so they could worry a little.

Roy tells me that even today if it happened again he would probably do it again because it was the proper thing to do - to take the dog home where it belongs.

Trip Home with John Bonner

Up to about the sixties, when you purchased a new automobile all you got were the two bumpers, the wheels, a body, and the steering wheel - everything else you wanted cost you extra. In this area and on north, there was a heater in the car most of the time. It cost you extra, but a car wouldn't sell without one, especially during the winter.

When I got out of the Coast Guard in 1954, I came home and got on the shrimp boat "*Agnes*" with my brother Charles and Glenwood Sadler. We headed for Marathon, Florida, to shrimp that winter; that was the going thing back then.

When Christmastime came and all of us wanted to come home, we got to looking' for a way to travel. Kenneth Robertson from Aurora had bought a brand new Dodge automobile the week before, but he wasn't coming home, so John Bonner Mayo from Campbell's Creek asked Kenneth if he could use his car. Kenneth told him he wasn't going to need it, so to go ahead and drive it up here.

There were a bunch of people from this area down there and most had their cars full by this time. John asked Charles, Glenwood, and me if we wanted to come up with him; we were glad to get the chance.

Rhondal Sadler called from Everglades (a small town on the west coast) and said he needed a way. John told him he had room and he could come with us.

Back then, a car you bought in south Florida came with no heater. It was warm year- round, so none was needed. It was never even thought of and there was not a heater in this car. (There was anti-freeze in the radiator; I guess that was standard.)

We left Marathon at about nine o'clock in the morning, and headed over to get Rhondal. It was a beautiful, hot sunny day; the weather up at home never entered our minds. John had two towels with him; I don't know why unless it was to wipe the sweat off the top of his head. (He had just a little hair above his ears on both sides, and the top was bald.) We picked up Rhondal about lunchtime and headed north. Towards sun-down, as we were headed on up into northern Florida, we passed through a cold front and it started to get cold. On into Georgia, it got cold-er and we went to putting on all the clothes we had with us and we still needed more.

About midnight, the windows went to icing up. John was driving, so he took one of his towels and started wiping the inside of the windshield to keep it from icing up. He rolled the other one up and put it on top of his head to keep it warm, and we kept coming north. Our breath was the warmest thing in the car and when the moisture from it hit the glass, it made ice. The windshield iced up so badly that it finally got down to about a four-inch hole for John to look out. He had to wipe it constantly to keep it from closing up; the other windows had iced-up completely. The temperature got down to about twenty degrees; the inside of that car was just about what it would be if you had put wheels on your old chest-type freezer, climbed in, and started driving it. Wall-to-wall ice.

About five o'clock the next morning, we got to Columbia, South Carolina. A man was opening up his station; he opened his big door and let us right on in so we could defrost the inside of the car and warm ourselves up.

After about an hour, we were ready to try it again. We could see out the windows, so we loaded up and headed north again. We had just gotten inside the town of Columbia on the main drag; it was just before daylight and the traffic was picking up. When a woman ahead of us stopped to let somebody out and then made a U-turn right in front of us, John laid on that horn; it made him mad. The horn blowing made the women mad. By the time she got all the way around, she had her window down and John had ours down. I guess you would have to call her "Mrs. Big." She was the type that thought: "Just wait until I get this thing turned around and I will fix you."

Well, we were ready to talk by the time she got abreast of us. John said, "Woman, what in the h--- was wrong with you?" She said, "I had my hand out." John said, "You had another part of your body out. Next time, I'm going to knock you off the road." He said more, too. She looked us over, put her car in gear, and squalled the tires taking off. Mrs. Big was moving out.

I can only imagine what was going on in that woman's mind when she looked inside at us: we had been up all night, with that towel wrapped around his head, John looked like one of these foreign snake charmers, my brother Charles had on an old Russian fur cap pulled down all the way, and I had on an old navy pea coat I brought out of the military with me; the collar was turned up all the way, and I had a cap on, so all you could see was my eyes and the end of my nose. Glenwood and Rhondal were bound up about the same way. I'm sure we didn't look to her like we were going to church.

It soon became daylight and started to warm up some; the windows didn't bother about icing up anymore, and we got home at about one o'clock in the evening.

142

When we started back down to Florida, we left so that we would be driving the coldest part of the trip during the daytime. It would have been a lot better had we done that on the way up.

Everyone Has a Mosquito Story and This is Mine !!!!!!!!

Ever since man has been on earth, he has been under the impression that giving blood is good for you. You can find accounts of our early-recorded history in which different kinds of rituals were used to "cleanse the body" or rid one of "old and bad blood." Some diseases were said to have been healed when people were bled.

With the best scientific information and all the modern-day technology, everything seems to point to the fact that these primitive methods - such as using leaches - perhaps did lead to cures or offer relief. I have in my hands a document distributed by the American Red Cross that's very interesting. It tells about a study done by the University of Kansas and the Eastern North Carolina Center in Greenville that states it is good to give blood, especially for men. Our blood often contains too much iron, and if we keep it and re-circulate it over and over, it could lead to a heart attack or other serious health problems after a period of time. If we give blood, the report says, our bodies will make new and better blood.

Mr. Kelly Watson Jr., who lives in New Bern, was born and raised in Lowland. He told me just the other day that he knew why folks lived longer in this area than other places. He said it's because we are giving blood to the mosquitoes all the time. I'm beginning to believe he's right! Mrs. Melissa Lewis lived in Lowland and was 102 years old when she passed away. Mr. Rob Popperwill of Lowland was also 102 when he died. My Uncle Roger Spencer was taken out of the house I now live in and put into a nursing home at one hundred years of age. Mr. Rufus Mason and his wife Lillian lived two houses from me and he was ninety-four when he passed away. Mrs. Ruth Mayo was ninety-eight when she died. Her sister, Mrs. Ada Mayo, is ninety-four. There is a Lupton family here on Goose Creek Island and the youngest is ninety-two, and is up and about and still lives at home. Mrs. Lillie Alcock is ninety-seven and she is a resident at Britthaven of Pamlico in Alliance. She still loves to sing. I know there are a lot of folks between ninety and a hundred years of age in this area, so there may be something to all of this!

After looking at this evidence, I find living here can't be all bad. Giving blood helps you in many ways. I prefer giving to the Red Cross because I'm helping someone, somewhere, but it's not always convenient. I guess I'll be glad when the mosquitoes come - a lot of them. All I have to do is walk out my door and the giving of blood will start immediately. You can give just as much as you want, too. All you have to do is go back inside when you think you have given enough and then you can start cleaning up and scratching all those bites.

The information I have also says you have to be seventeen to start giving blood and you have to be in good health. It's not that way when you use the "mosquito method." You can start giving blood the very moment you come into the world. If your parent takes you outside in the summer, those pesky insects will bite you whether you are sick or not - it really doesn't matter to them. They don't discriminate and they bite everything that has blood - whether it's living or dead (Although I think they prefer the warm-blooded to the cold-blooded.) I haven't checked that out yet, so I'm not really sure that it's so. The species (wild animals, horses, mules, dogs, cats and rats) and color doesn't make a bit of difference to a mosquito. It doesn't matter whether you are moving or standing still, they'll go after that blood. I think running might help if you have given all you plan to!

The information I have also says you can give blood every fifty-six days, but here on Goose Creek Island, you can give blood every day, especially at sunup and sundown.

I heard my daddy say one time that he had seen the mosquitoes so thick that it took two men to plow with a mule – one man to work the plow and another one with a tow bag to beat the mosquitoes off the mule to keep him from laying down and rolling over. The harnesses would be all tangled up if that happened.

Around 1955, mosquitoes were bad everywhere, including in the middle of the Pamlico Sound. Some of the boats had smoke pots going on the back decks of their boats so the men could work. They were probably eight to ten miles from land.

Mosquitoes will get into the house and bite you and continue biting you after you go to bed. You hear one buzzing and can't think about sleeping until that mosquito lands on you and you swat it. That buzzing sounds like a jet plane going overhead when you're in bed. You stay very alert and wait for that sucker to land and bite. Sometimes you have to turn on a light and get up in order to deal with it. Before electricity, there were no lights to turn on, so you had to make a choice of trying to keep swatting at the mosquito in the dark until he was killed, or letting him land on you.

Now, we don't need a mass migration down to this area to give blood in hopes that it will make you live longer. We just don't have all the things that are needed to handle a whole lot of people. Our roads would become all blocked up. They are not wide enough for cars to park on both sides and have their doors open so the mosquitoes can get in to bite!

It's better to stay where you live and go to the Red Cross Bloodmobile when it's in your area to give blood about every sixty days. That way, you are helping someone, somewhere, as well as yourself. You'll get a mini-physical and find out the condition of your blood in the process.

I am looking for Kelly Watson, Jr. and Roy Cahoon to move on back down this way any time now, so they can be here for the beginning of summer. If they don't figure out a way to give blood, I just might outlive both of them.

Manning Lupton's Lost Stool

In 1962, my brother, Charles, owned a shrimp boat called the *Chris F.* It was about seventy-five feet long with the pilothouse on the bow - almost all shrimp boats are built this way. Charles decided that he wanted to make some changes on it. He didn't like the pilothouse where it was, and it didn't carry enough fuel to suit him, the way it was arranged. He hired Royce Spain to do the carpentry work and Manning Lupton to measure and build new fuel tanks, and for what other welding work that needed to be done, me and his crew.

Royce started to build a new pilothouse on the stern and we began to remove the equipment out of the old pilothouse, so we could go to removing it.

Manning had to measure the area under the bow pilothouse so he could build the additional fuel tank that was to go there. The steel had to be cut and put down inside of the boat in pieces and welded up in place - there was no way to get them down inside the boat after they were built in his shop.

The pieces of steel came and we helped him get them down inside of the boat, enough to build the first tank. We held the sides in place so he could tack it together and to the bottom. Then he would take his stool and crawl inside and sit while he welded up the inside. This took about three days before he would come out and put the top on and weld up the outside.

The first tank done and put in place, we helped him take the steel down for the second tank, and he tacked it together. After about four days of welding - both inside and out - he called us to help him put the top on. We went down and helped him and he tacked it in place, then we came on out and left him. After he had been welding about four hours, he hollered out to us on deck and wanted to know if we had seen his stool; he couldn't find it. By this time, he had come out from below with just his head sticking out, waiting for our answer. He said what we were all thinking, that I had left that stool in the tank. He started to crawl out, head-

ing for his shop. He said he was going to get his torch and cut the top back off. Charles told him to come on back and leave it in there, to continue to weld on it. He didn't think it would ever be any problem, so Manning left it.

A few years later, Charles sold that boat to some people in Texas. Some years after that, I heard it burned up and sank in the Gulf of Mexico. So if sometime in the future, that boat is removed from the Gulf for some reason, if they open up that tank, I'm sure they will be surprised to find Manning's stool.

*Manning in front
of his shop*

Mr. Robert Hopkins's Mower

In the early fifties, they started making a lawn mower with a little engine sitting on its end on top of the frame with the shaft going through the frame and a blade underneath. It was the first time a mower had been put on the old rotary-type push mower.

You had to mix the oil with the gas and the mixture had to be right in order for it to work right. Each mower came with a pull cord – there was a little pulley on top for you to wrap it around to start it, and there were no recoils on them. When they started fairly quickly, there was no problem, but if they didn't, you could soon have blisters on your hands from cranking them.

One time when Daddy was walking by Mr. Robert Hopkins's place, Mr. Hopkins had his mower out, trying to start it. He had cranked on it with that pull cord until there were blisters on his hands. He was sitting down when Daddy walked up; he wasn't in a very good mood. He told Daddy that he had made a mistake. When he got that mower out, he should have gotten his ax out, too, because if he had it handy, he would have gone and used it. By the time he could find it and get back to that mower, he had cooled off, he said, so he was letting it set for a while before he tried it again. Next time I take the mower out, the ax comes too.

Clyde Smith and the Bear

In the sixties, Clyde Smith had a thirty-foot oyster boat he worked by himself. It had a small cabin on it, so he could stay overnight on it if he wanted to - one fold-down bunk and a small cook stove. It had what was called an awning that started at the back of the cabin and went a little ways back with two windows in the front of it. It gave him added protection from the weather.

One day, Clyde was working over in Carteret County, up in Long Bay. He had caught some oysters and a good number of flounders that he threw under the stern to get them out of the way as he worked. When night came, he went a little further up the bay and put the bow of the boat to the bank and put his anchor out. Then he went to the stern and took his pole and pushed the boat around until its side was against the bank.

He stuck it down to hold it like that. He decided to clean a couple of those flounders to eat for his supper with the small knife he had in his pocket.

After he had done all of that, he dropped down his bunk and went to bed. Some time during the night, something happened to his boat. It rolled over on its side, just about rolling him out of his bunk, with pots, pans, and buckets beating all together as they fell. Then the boat straightened back up. Clyde was thinking, what happened? Still half asleep, he decided to slip ahead on his bunk

Clyde Smith

until he could get a hold of the front hatch, which was on top of the cabin at the front edge, and pull it open just enough to get his head out to look around. When he did and he looked through the windows of the awning, he saw about a seven hundred-pound bear in the stern of his boat, eating his flounders. He got down and closed that hatch, quick!

"My gracious, what am I going to do? I don't think the back door is closed good, and it's not hooked, and I've not got a gun or even a knife to deal with this bear." Clyde said the bear was pulling cans out from under the stern and throwing them all around to get to all the fish. Clyde thought about the fried fish that was leftover from supper that was sitting on the cook stove inside the cabin. He thought, if the bear smells those fried fish, he might come in here. He knew that the back door was no match if that bear wanted to come in, or even the back of the whole cabin - he would wipe it out with one swipe. Clyde just didn't know what he was going to do.

After the bear had eaten all of his fish, he stood up on his back feet and looked around. He must have been seven feet tall, with some white on his throat. He got up on the stern - just about turning the boat over as

149

he jumped - and headed for shore. I'm sure Clyde was one relieved man when he saw that bear go.

Clyde told me his weight was about three hundred pounds at that time, but he knew he wasn't a match for that bear. He also said that he learned something from it: he didn't ever tie up his boat alongside the bank again.

I think about the song "The Preacher and The Bear". The last two lines in it are: "Lord if you can't help me, for goodness sake - don't you help that bear." That would work here.

My Award-winning Lie

In 1972, Pamlico County was one hundred years old and there was a general feeling throughout the county that we should have a celebration. The third week of April was selected. We had it at the high school in Bayboro; it was a beautiful week of weather and a big success.

It went on all week long, with parades, contests of all kinds for the old and young during the day, and a play that went on at night with skits in it with local talent. It was narrated by Mr. Jack Brinson, who recalled the "firsts" of all the new things that had made their way to the county and which are now part of the history of the county, and how families had reacted to them. Some military history was also put on. Many people from all over the county were involved.

The men in the play grew beards, and some of the women dressed as women did during that period; there was gospel singing from the churches all week and there were fireworks on Saturday night. A big gospel sing was put on at the school grounds on Sunday evening; groups from all over the county sang.

I was in the play and I entered two contests: the first was for the Van Dyke beard I grew (I won the trophy); the other was the Liar's Contest. I won that too, so I guess it made me the biggest liar in the county at that time. This contest was for amateurs (if some of the folks I know had entered, I wouldn't have had a chance).

I looked everywhere, did a lot of reading, and couldn't find anything I liked until the day before the contest when I ran into Metta Swindell. She asked me if I had found a lie yet. I told her no, that I was considering canceling out of the contest. She handed me a piece of paper with a lie on it and told me to read it - I might like it. I liked it the first time I read it; it was my kind of lie. Here it is:

When I bought my home here in Hobucken, it was on a half-acre lot. After a few years, I decided to have a garden, so I needed more land. I bought another half-acre lot directly back of it, which had grown up in vines and trees.

One of the first things I had to do was to clear it off; my two boys and I went to work on it. One day when I was working out there using the hoe, I ran across a snake. I chopped at it several times trying to kill it, and before I finally did, it reached up and bit the wooden part of the hoe handle. I threw the snake into the woods after I was sure it was dead and laid the hoe down by the side of the garden. It was late in the day, so I went on into the house.

The next morning when I came out and saw that hoe handle, I couldn't believe what I saw. The poison from that snake had gone into the wood and the wood was growing. It had grown all night. It was six feet across the end of it and still growing. I decided to get it to the sawmill and saw it up into lumber so I could build me a shop out of the wood, which I did. When I got the lumber back from the sawmill, my two boys and went to work. In about a week, I had a fifteen-by-twenty foot building. I was real proud of our work, and one evening I stood out there admiring that building.

I decided that in order to make our work look real good and add some class to it, I had to paint it. I got some tan paint to make it blend with my house, and one evening I started to paint it. I finished up just before sundown, cleaned everything up, and went into the house. There was a big surprise when I opened that back door the next morning: that paint had gone into the wood and neutralized the poison and that building had shrunk up until it wasn't any bigger than a shoe box. I was back to square one.

I don't know how long that title is good for. If it's until the next centennial celebration, I have a choice to make: to either tell the same lie, or find a new one.

(The trophy was presented to me by Mr. Mathew Prescott.)

My liar's trophy

Our Wild Friends

We have an abundance of bears on the Island this year. We live close to a wildlife viewing area, but we don't have to go there to see wildlife. In most cases, all we have to do is look out the window. They are so plentiful, people talk to them when they get in the way.

There is a group of ladies that walks along our roads in the early mornings and evenings. For a lot of different reasons - I wouldn't dare list any of them - some walk at night when it's cooler. I have heard them laughing and talking when they go walking by my house.

We have a young man named Greg Jones here in our neighborhood who has a boom box in his car. I know when he goes by, because my entire house vibrates. One night a couple of months ago, I heard him coming down the road real slow. When he got to my house, he sped up a little as he passed.

I could tell by the actions of my dog Lassie that things outside were not as usual. Lassie was standing up, sniffing, like something was far off, and turning her head side to side and lifting her nose high. She made no attempt to go outside; she just walked around smelling and appeared to be very nervous. Just after Greg passed my house, he stopped, and I could hear people talking loud outside. He soon drove off. In about ten minutes, I got a phone call from one of the ladies telling me there was a bear in front of my house, near the road at the edge of my yard. Greg had seen it and when he saw those ladies walking towards him, he stopped and told them about the bear. He told them to get in the car - they didn't need to go any further. They got in and he took them home. They told me the bear went down alongside my house, heading for the woods in the back. I couldn't get Lassie to go outside.

I have driven through towards Lowland on the Schoolhouse Road and I have seen people parked along the side of the road in those open fields, looking toward the woods. Most of the time, you can see bears in the fields. Sometimes, there are six or more playing and eating the crops.Not too long ago, Alice Ledford got to walking in the early mornings on the Lowland Road before she went to work. Many of those mornings, she saw bears in the fields and woods as she walked along. One morning when she was walking - heading home - there was a bear on the road between her and her home. She stopped and waited on him to get across.

John Ireland was on his way to the Marina and when he saw her, he stopped to find out what was wrong. She told him, so John stayed with her as she walked home.

A few mornings after that, she was walking towards Lowland way, and was almost to Spring's Creek, when she saw a bear just off the road a little ways. She went on to Springs Creek Bridge and turned around, and when she got up to where the bear was, he had decided to get on the road with her. When she stopped walking, he stood up on his back legs. He was close to eight feet tall; she was close enough to talk to him. She told him that he had to get off the road so she could go home. He finally did, and she got on home.

One of the last homes to be built on this island was Roy and Mae Lupton's. It's a nice, big two-story brick home on the main road here in Hobucken. A few years after it was built, Roy had a swimming pool put in right behind it, with a partial fence around it.

One Saturday morning, Roy got up. Some of his help wasn't going to be at work that day at his store, so he got his daughter, Jennifer, to go and help him. They had both eaten breakfast and Roy had gotten ready, so he sat down with the newspaper to wait for Jennifer. She was in her bedroom in the back and heard the water splashing around in the swimming pool. She thought, I hope Daddy hasn't decided to go swimming this morning; we don't have enough time for that. When she went to the window, she got a surprise - there was a bear taking a morning dip in the pool. She hollered for her daddy and he jumped up and went out the back door onto the deck. When the bear saw him, he started trying to get out. He was in the deep end; there was nothing for him to put his back feet on to help him get out. He finally worked down the side of the pool until he got his feet to touch bottom.

Roy went to talking to the bear as he was working down the side of the pool towards the shallow end. He told him that he had to get out of the pool; that Roy didn't want him in it. He said the bear had to find another place to swim. The bear finally got out and headed for the woods. Roy has a bunch of hunting dogs penned up, not too far from his house. He said they were standing stiff-footed, their bristles standing up - all of them barking, wanting to get out to get a hold of that bear.

Old Windmill - North Side of Jones Bay

As long as I can remember, I have heard about the old windmill and gristmill operation that was on the north side of Jones Bay. The area is called Windmill Point. I was also told that the old stones from this mill were still at the site, which are all woods today.

The winter before last, after I retired and got interested in the history of this area, I decided to go and see if I could find them. Going in from the main road looked bad. I tried several times in different places, but it was too over-grown with briars and vines and ditches to make it. After several attempts, I gave up on finding them from the roadway.

Mr. Roland Leary had a small fiberglass skiff in his yard. I decided to try to go in from the Jones Bay side. One day, I asked him if I could use it. He told me I could, anytime I decided to go.

Odell Spain's drawing of a domed windmill

One morning when it was not too cold and there was no wind blowing, I got my electric trolling motor and the skiff, and headed for Jones Bay. I put it over at Doll's Creek and went to going up the Bay. With so many ditches dug, I didn't know which was the right one. I wasn't sure just where they were.

The first ditch came to a dead end, so I had to back out. The next ditch went a little further in, but it, too, hooked onto a smaller ditch and made a turn.

The third ditch looked different after I started up it. There were old oyster shells on the side of it and the remains of old stakes where skiffs had been tied years ago. Scrub oaks were hanging over it in places. I went up it about as far as I could go. Then I got out and went to walking a short distance to the woods. Just inside the woods, I saw a raised place

He believes that the bear was heading for the woods and ran up with his dogs, so he changed his course and headed for the three-foot opening in Roy's wood fence. When he went through it running at full speed, the swimming pool was just too close for him to stop before going in it.

Roy said that he had been thinking of putting up a sign as a joke, saying that there would be "no bare swimming" in his pool. He is still thinking about it, but he will have to change the wording a little to include this kind of bear, too.

P.S. This is not history - it happened this summer, 1997

THE FISHING LIFE

Captain Edwin Ireland

Sailboats were the only way of life here many years ago - all shipping was done by water and communities were made up around creeks in the area. The remains of old sailboats and docks on some of these creeks are evidence of this by-gone area. Sometimes, people took their home apart and moved it - and their families - by boat. My daddy told me that as a boy, he had seen forty to fifty sailboats anchored in Jones Bay during bad weather. Their crews came ashore every night to go to preaching at the Alliance Hall and visit friends.

When I came along, sailboats were on their way out, but there were still three in the family: George Lupton had a bateau named the *Lois S.*, Wilbur Watson had a bateau named the *Hattie Lloyd*, and Daddy and Uncle Fred had a Sharpie named the *Virgil* (Wilbur and George married my two oldest sisters, Esther and Valeria).

These men went to getting these boats ready for oystering in August. That meant scraping and painting and getting them hauled out at Oriental at Will Dixon Railways.

The year of 1938, Wilbur was getting the *Hattie Lloyd* ready to go to Oriental. His brother Plum was getting his bateau the *Robert Cole* ready, so they decided to go to Oriental together. Plum's wife Lillie went, and Plum got Capt. Ed Ireland to go with him. With nothing but sail power, you had to start a few days early; you didn't know how long it might take you to get there. My sister Valeria went with Wilbur.

They left Eastman's Creek dock (a branch off of Goose Creek, Pamlico River) about midday, coming through the Intracoastal Waterway. There was a light wind blowing and they were moving slow. They got through the drawbridge heading on towards Gale's Creek, Bay River. Thunder squalls began to make up and when they got into Gale's Creek, one of them was going to hit them, so they dropped the sails and put out the anchor.

After the squall passed, every bit of the wind fell out; it was slick calm, and hot. They couldn't move and night was coming on, as well as mosquitoes coming aboard. With no screens and no insect killer, they had to get inside the cabin and close it up; the mosquitoes were eating them up. Valeria had an old shirt that they put in a bucket and set afire to make a smoke to run them out. She said it only ran them into the corners and as soon as it died down, they were right back biting.

They tried to sleep a little; Wilbur finally got up and said it must not be too long before daylight. Valeria told him to look at her watch; it was up there on a shelf. Wilbur made a light and looked. It was only ten after ten, so they lay back down. It was a long and miserable night.

When it did finally come daylight, there was some wind blowing from the west so they pulled anchor, raised the sails, and went on to Oriental.

On a Saturday evening, Mr. Will Dixon pulled the *Hattie Lloyd* up on the railway. Wilbur and the railway crew worked on it until sundown and were going to paint it Monday morning. The *Robert Cole* would be next to come up; Capt. Ed and Plum were doing everything they could to get it ready.

On Sunday morning, Wilbur had just gotten out on the deck when he heard Plum hollering and running up the dock saying, "Wilbur, Wilbur, Capt. Ed's dead." "What's that, Plum?" Wilbur said. Plum said again, "Capt. Ed's dead." Wilbur said, "Are you sure?" Plum said, "Yes, he's deader than a hammer, down there in the forepeak." Wilbur said, "Let me get down, Plum, and I'll go down there and see if Ed's dead." Wilbur went down there, right on down into the forepeak. Capt. Ed's eyes were still open, and Wilbur determined that sure enough, Capt. Ed was dead.

They decided to go up the street to a grocery store and call to Fred Lewis's store at Lowland and get word to the family so somebody could come and get his body. They had to call the coroner to come down to pronounce him dead.

There were a lot of people living in Oriental who had moved out of this area, so there were a lot of family connections and friends who lived there. As the word got out about Capt. Ed, it wasn't long before about half of the town was down at the railway.

Mr. Stilly Hopkins, Uncle Joe Hudnell, and his wife, Mary Lizzer, were there. When she looked in, she told Mr. Stilly to go down there and close Capt. Ed's eyes. Mr. Stilly told her he didn't open them, and he wasn't going down there.

It was about midday when the coroner showed up and not much later when Mr. Fred Lewis came up with his truck. He had put a cot in the back of it and got Capt. Ed's body and brought it home. Capt. Ed was buried the next day in the Watson Cemetery at Lowland; he died Aug. 28, 1938.

Captain Edwin Ireland
(Capt. Ed)

Long Haul Netting

I used to hear my daddy say that things had changed so much in his lifetime, he was born too soon. I realize now what he was talking about. Being raised up in a family that the way of life was commercial fishing, I see how much this industry has changed.

The way to catch fish in the twenties and thirties and earlier, was pound netting. It was hard work the entire year. They would shad fish in the winter at Pamlico Point. This required a lot of work getting poles out of the woods, taking the bark off, and getting them to the river and nets where they put them in the bottom using a maul. The entrance of Pamlico River was the best and closest place; it was called Pamlico Point.

Being at Pamlico Point, it was a lot easier to go up Oyster Creek at Lowland to get the stakes they used. One year, they asked a man to get some stakes off his land. He told them if they took the land along with the stakes, they could do it, so he wrote them out a deed for it.

In the spring of the year, the shad nets were taken up. They would work about three weeks in the woods getting new stakes and taking them to Pamlico Point to be put out with the summer nets. This was the best way at that time to catch fish. It was just the fish that came along the shores they could catch.

Then the idea of putting one of these automobile engines in a boat came along, making big changes. The boats had more power. They could be bigger, too, so the way of catching fish changed. You could go out away from shore with these powerboats and pull the nets with them, not wait for the fish to come to you. Sometimes, these engines were not dependable. They would only last a few years, because they were cooled with salt water and the rust would eat them up. But they were better than the old way.

This was "long haul netting" as it was called, and it came with its own set of problems. First of all, it took two boats, two net skiffs, and seven men to make it work - three men on each powerboat and one to run the

Haul netting in 1945. From left to right: Ralph Whitfield, Mayhue Norman, Bert Roberson, Virgil Carawan, Lee Mayo.

run-boat. (This was the boat that carried the fish in to the fish house.)

There were eight nets: each powerboat had a net skiff in tow with four nets in each, consisting of two, two hundred yard wing nets (they were the biggest mesh), one junior net (a smaller mesh), and one back net - the smallest net, which was about one and a half inch mesh and about 150 yards long. Plus, one carried what was called a bunt net. These nets had a pole on each end of them called a staff, and the staffs were tied together to make them one continuous net.

Weather had to be closely watched. The wind went to falling out about midnight, so by two a.m., everybody was ready to go. The decision had to be made then whether to go into the Sound or stay in one of the bays, basing this on what they thought the weather was going to do. If the weather turned bad and you were in the Sound, you had to try and get the nets up, or leave them with buoys on them and come back after the weather improved to get them.

When they finally chose where they were going to lay out, they started out no later than three a.m., using just the sounding pole to steer by. (I wrote about this in another story.) When they got to where they wanted to be, the two boats - each going in opposite directions - would come by one another. The men in the skiffs would hand the staff to the other. They would tie the back net staffs together and the boats would continue with the laying out, going in opposite directions. When they got them just about all out, the captain would hand them the end of the hawser that was hooked on the powerboat, and they would tie it to the last staff just before it went over the stern. When it was all done, the hawser came tight, and they sped up the engine to go pulling, heading for the shallow water. This could take from one hour to four hours or more, depending where you were and how far it was to footing bottom.

During this time, you had breakfast: hot coffee or water, fresh eggs (fried if it was calm, or scrambled if the boat was rolling bad), hand-sliced, molded bacon, and made from scratch - hot biscuits.

Footing bottom was about, or just above, waist deep water. Just before they got the ends they were pulling on to shallow water, the men would get into the skiffs and leave the powerboat and go to paddling on in. They would stop about half way between the two pull boats on the edge of shallow water and stick a stake in the bottom. It was called the footing stake; this would be where the powerboats would take the ends of the nets to, and tie them when they got ashore.

The next thing was cutting-out. The pull boat would take the skiff in tow and head offshore to a buoy on the end of the wing net. Here, they would separate the nets and tie the skiff to the junior net. Then the captain would come back by, throwing the end of the hawser to them, and they would tie it to the junior net. As the pull boat pulled this net toward shore, the men in the skiff would be taking the wing nets up as they went. When this was complete, they would start back to do the same thing with the junior net, except the skiff with the bunt net would start at the footing stake and put the bunt net over as they headed out. (This was a short net and small mesh.) When they got to the back net buoy, they would pick it up, tie to the back net, and do the same process as they had done with the wing nets. Except this time, when they got to the end on the side the bunt net was put out on, they would tie the end of the back net to it, and the other side would continue to start (pulling by) by the stake, as far as he could go. Most of the time, the first back net and part of the next one, if he didn't get cut off by the shore line or the water to shallow to float in, by this time, one pull boat anchored and everybody was going overboard. When the boat had to stop, we had to pull the nets by hand.

This was no picnic. It was dangerous; usually the captain would go to the footing stake and stand in the entrance of where the nets were coming together. The idea was to keep the bottom line tight on the bottom. Whatever is in the pond, you are exposed to. My daddy got stung in the leg by a stingray one year. He felt it, and when he pulled his leg up, the stingray was still hooked to it. Tearing it was worse, until it broke off from the stingray. The crew had to pull it out of his leg with a pair of pliers. Then they had to bring him in to the doctor. Some years, the sea nettles were bad. It was pure torture – you had to cover a big area of bottom with these nets, and bring them together at this point. Sometimes the water would be nothing but hot jelly, and you had to get overboard in it. This would separate the men from the boys here - a lot of men lasted only a week, sometimes just a day, at haul netting. Mr. Walter Sadler (ninety-two years old) told me that one year he was helping to foot a net and he made a vow to himself, "when I get ashore, if another sea nettle stings me, he is going to come out of the water to do it."

The years I worked at it, we had clothes that were made out of canvas that would keep most parts of them from stinging our bodies, but the water would be hot - they were stinging everything they touched. We would still be burning, and when it was over, our wrist and hands were blistered.

Putting out the bunt net. That's Ralph Whitfield on the left, Lee Mayo overboard

My brother, Thomas, said when he was haul netting in the thirties, they had pants only to the waist. The last year he worked haul netting was 1937. They worked on shares, and he had worked seven weeks and hadn't seen a dime, so he went to working on freight boats. Before trawling or pollution, you had years that a living couldn't be made from haul netting. For whatever reason, there were no fish to catch in the Sound by any method at that time.

You keep pulling one side of the nets around until the end of the bunt net goes by. At that point, the skiff is brought in and you start to take it up in the skiff. The bunt net is small mesh and very baggy; you keep pulling the bottom line until it gets all the way across and under the fish, making the pond smaller. At that time, the run boat is moved until it is alongside, the footing stake is pulled up and put inside the railing, and then the net is pulled in the skiff until you can't pull it any more. The man on the run boat is ready with a basket hooked on block and fall – it's at this point you know how you have done - and the bailing of fish starts into the run boat until they are all bailed out. I have helped load boats this way and I also have helped when it only made one bale or less.

After this is complete, the bunt net is put back overboard to wash it, and the men get in the skiffs and go to taking up the back nets. Usually there is some fish stuck into them, depending on how good the catch was. It's usually where a man makes up his mind what kind of fish he is going to eat for his dinner. You eat fish or nothing; this is the only choice you have.

Some days, if you got done early enough and didn't have nothing on the haul, you would move on and make another haul before sundown, usually up in one

An old net skiff

of the bays. If it was too late, and your nets were in good shape, everybody headed into the harbor.

After they stopped these engines, they usually didn't want to start them anymore because they had to get in the cabin with them to sleep - one over the top of it, the other two on each side. There were times when a thunder squall would come up during the night and you would have to move to another harbor. After you were anchored, you went back in the bunk. Can you imagine how that was: it would be raining, all the windows closed up tight, and you trying to sleep around a hot pile of iron?

The last long haul netting that was done here was in 1986 by Michael Lewis of Lowland. There is some haul netting going on Carteret County today and a few who are just using half of the rig and one boat in this area, I'm told.

A lot of evenings, there would be two or three crews tied up together. There would be some big fishing hauls made, to hear them talk. Some of the world's worst problems would be solved during the evening among the men, and politics was serious with some of them. Hundred-dollar bets were not uncommon on some of the issues. (I never saw any money.) Sometimes, hats were taken off and somebody would invite another on the stern to straighten the issue out. (Never saw any licks passed.)

This came about, passed through, and was gone from this area in my lifetime.

The Trawler *Sara J.*

The *Sara J.* was built at Belhaven in the mid forties, along with the *Randelyn.* It was built out of the best material available. The framing was on about eight-inch centers; the planking was two inches thick or more; and the keel was fastened in such a way that it extended up through the bottom to the deck in the stern sections. It also had two, forty- foot rolling chocks on the bottom. (These were shaped like little keels fastened close to the outer edge of the bottom. The idea was they would hold the water on each side and it would make the boat roll slower.)

It was styled after the New England-type boats - the pilot-house was on the stern and went all the way through and was part of the stern. It was an extremely well built and strong boat of eighty-five feet, built to work in the ocean in the fishing business. This boat was a moneymaker - just about all the captains who worked

The Sara J. at dock

it over the years did well with it. Not everybody wanted to work it, because the man in charge had to be above average in seamanship. This boat needed nine feet of water to float in; with the inlets here along the Pamlico Sound being so shallow, the captain had to be on his toes just to go in and out of them.

The last captain to work the *Sara J.* was Ernest Mayo from Mesic. He was considered to be one of the best captains and fisherman on the east coast. On the boat with him were Lonnie Carawan, Richard Carpenter, Mose Manning, and Frank Leary (the only one left of this crew).

When a fisherman finds a school of fish, he likes to work as long as possible to catch them; fish move and you can't find them later on. In the ocean, there are a lot of unknowns you have to deal with: the weather, tides, ship wrecks (and other things on the bottom that tear the nets up), and making sure you keep out of the way of merchant ships or they might run over you. (It has happened.) To make things worse, after you decide to come in to get to the market, first you have to deal with the inlets in this area.

One time, Ernest and this crew had been out for fourteen days; it had been a good trip. They had about three hundred boxes of bass and two hundred and fifty boxes of flounder on board. They had worked until they had just enough fuel to get to the dock when they headed in.

They got to the bar at Organ Inlet just about dark. It was rough and it was a bad time to try to come in, but they didn't have enough fuel to go to Chesapeake Bay or around Cape Hatteras and they couldn't stay in the ocean any longer, so they had to try it.

The deep water in these inlets shifts back and forth, so the buoys you go out with may not be in the deepest water when you come back, but that's all you've got to go by. The *Sara J.* was drawing eleven feet or more with all the fish on board, so they needed to stay in the deepest water, if possible.

Ernest got the buoys lined up and headed over the bar. They hit bottom, but were able to back off without any damage to the boat. They tried again and hit bottom again. With the tide running like it was, they couldn't get clear anymore. The boat turned broadside in the breakers and hit the bottom hard, so Ernest put it in forward gear and opened the throttle to push it farther up in shallow water to keep it from hitting the bottom so hard again. A big breaker hit the Sara J. broadside and knocked her over on her side, pushing one of the rolling chocks up through the bottom. Water started to come in, fast.

Frank started the pumps - a three-inch, a two-inch, and two inch-and-a-quarter pumps. In a short time, the water was almost knee-deep in the engine room and they seemed to be holding it at that level.

Eleven o'clock was a tide change. Frank told Ernest he didn't believe they could hold down the water after the tide went to running, so he had to decide whether to shut down the engine or let the water do it. Frank said the water was rising in the engine room and was going to go over the batteries before long.

The Coast Guard station was in sight from where they were, so Ernest called and told them the situation. He said he was going to need some help. He also told them that the batteries were going under the water and that he was going to shut down the engine (which meant that the lights would shut down, too). They asked him if they had any kind of flashlights on board; he said they did. They told him to shine them toward the station if the crew was going to have to get off. By this time, the breakers were getting big.

At about two a.m., two self-bailing Coast Guard boats went out to try to get them. When the breakers hit them, they rolled completely over, straightened up, and tried again. They finally gave up. They couldn't get to them; it was too rough.

About good daylight, a helicopter came and hovered over them. When it dropped down a man bucket, the first man crawled in and was taken to the station and put out. Then it came right back for another. Three of the crew got off with no trouble. When they came the fourth time, they had a problem getting the bucket down to the boat, but they finally did. Ernest held on to it while Frank got in. Ernest told Frank to tell the Coast Guard not to come back for him; he wasn't going ashore.

When Ernest turned the bucket loose, it moved over the open water just clear of the side of the boat and stopped. When they started to raise it up, the winch quit working. Frank said he could see them up there working on it, but each time they tried it, he dropped a little. There was a big breaker coming. Frank said he hadn't paid much attention to the breakers before, but just before it got to him, the bucket dropped him about six feet. The top of the breaker hit him and he got wet from the shoulders down. They motioned to him that they were taking him ashore in the bucket; he was hanging thirty to forty feet under it.

The helicopter lifted the bucket up until it was about twenty feet above the water and headed in. When they got to the beach, Frank got real concerned because the power line running on the beach was about the same level as the bucket. He thought, "I sure hope the pilot hasn't forgotten me under here. If I go through those lines, I will look like sliced cheese." Just before they got to them, the pilot lifted him up until he had plenty of clearance over the lines. They went to the station and set the bucket down. A man came running out and got Frank out of it, and then the helicopter set down alongside. Frank told them not to go back for Ernest, because he wasn't coming ashore.

Ernest stayed on the *Sara J.* all day Sunday and Sunday night. On Monday, the weather had got a little better, so they went out to him in a boat. The stern and the back of the pilothouse were gone. Ernest was in the front part of the pilothouse and decided to come ashore. I'm sure that was one of the most difficult decisions he ever had to make; when a captain has to leave his ship, it's the worst time in his life.

Ernest told the local fisherman to go out and get all the fish they could out of the boat. There was about an hour and half at tide change during which they could go to it and get them.

A company out of Virginia came down and salvaged everything they could off the *Sara J.*, including the engine. Usually, when a wood boat goes ashore on the beach, there's no sign of it twenty-four hours later; it's gone to pieces and washed away. Not the *Sara J.* She was still visible for a year or longer after the accident.

The Coast Guard presented Frank with a Certificate of Heroism and a set of wings for his riding in the bucket ashore; he has them today at his home.

Ernest and Frank went back to work fishing on the *Clara* and worked a few more years together.

Sara J. at Organ Inlet

P.S. This is from Frank Leary; it was to be the last one. Some of it I got from him while he was in the hospital. He is back home now, and I understand they told him there was nothing else they could do for him. I could tell he was weaker than when I got the following story. Don't know how much longer he will be with us.

Pictures are from the book put out by the town of Vandemere.

The *Randelyn*

In the 1940's there was a big transition going on in the way a man made a living on the water. Powerboats were taking over and the sail-boats that had been a way of life for centuries were fading away.

At first, the boats that were used to make a living with were small, but as shrimping began to come about, they began to get bigger. I shrimped with my brother Charles the summer of 1948 and most of the boats were the same ones that were used to oyster with during the winter; they were thirty-two feet or smaller. The few bigger boats that were used were used in the ocean to catch fish.

A lot of bigger boats were being built all around Pamlico Sound to use in the shrimping business. There had been no set pattern as to which type of boat would be the best for this industry. In New England, all the boats working offshore in the ocean had the pilothouse on the stern, with the engine under it. Down this way, the boats being built for the shrimp industry had the engine under the pilothouse on the bow.

The *Randelyn* was built about 1945 at Belhaven by Clyde Potter. It was considered a big boat for the times; it was about eighty feet in length. I don't know who designed it, but it seems like a compromise between the northern boats and the boats of this area because the pilot-house was on the stern and the engine was toward the bow. It seemed ill-arranged, at the time.

Folks around this area tell the story that while this boat was being built, an old black lady came down to the docks one day and asked Clyde for a few fish to eat. Clyde told her he didn't have any, so on her way out she laid her hand up on one of the ribs that was in it, bowed her head, and seemed to be praying. She told the men building it, "I'm putting a curse on this boat. It will never make any money for the owner of it." Whether this is so or not, I don't know. But as I tell you about this one story in the life of the *Randelyn*, it may make you wonder.

From the beginning, based on what I know about it and what I've been told, there were always problems with it. Nobody seemed to be able to work it with any success; you make a little with it this week, and then something would break down and it would take what you had made to fix it and get it going again. A lot of different captains tried to work it and they all had about the same problem. My brother, Charles, tried to work it in the spring of 1955, but he soon gave it up; the up-keep to make it work seemed too much for what could be produced with it.

Byron Hopkins from Hobucken, who was liv- ing at Marathon, Florida, came up and took it over. He fished it awhile offshore here, but did- n't make much with it. About two weeks before Christmas, he decided to take it to Florida and try shrimping with it. On the boat with him at that time were Kenneth Pate, Ralph Smithwick of Bayboro, and Frank Leary. (He's the only one still living of this crew, and the one who filled me in with the details.)

Bryon Hopkins

The smaller shrimp boats going south went down the Intracoastal Waterway most of the time, going into the ocean at Cape Fear River, if the weather permitted, and following the coastline on south. With these big- ger boats, they went out at Morehead-Beaufort inlet and set a straight course for Foley Rocks, just south of Miami. Going this route saved a lot of time, but with the coastline curving the way it does, you're a long way offshore at about the middle of trip, should anything go wrong.

Byron and his crew teamed up with the *Ethel V. Stowman.* This boat was about one hundred feet long and the crew was from Belhaven. They went out of the inlet about two in the morning. Byron set up four-hour watches for the crew. The weather was not too bad, and everything was going fine.

About sundown, a cold front passed them. The wind picked up from the northwest and went to blowing from forty to fifty knots. It was getting rough and cold. The waves got so rough that the *Randelyn* lost sight of the *Stowman;* the visibility got down to a few hundred feet.

Ralph was the engineer, so he decided to pump the boat out before lying down. There were gasoline pumps in the engine room and one under the pilothouse floor. The pumps in the engine room had to be gassed up from the deck, so he went forward and got the can out to fill them up. Because it was so rough, he broke the spout out of the can. He then went down and got a service can (an open-top can with a flexible spout you see around service stations) and filled it up with gas to fill the pump under the pilothouse floor.

The butane stove to keep the pilothouse warm was on when Ralph came in carrying that can of gas. Frank was steering; Kenneth was supposed to start at eight o'clock. Byron was in the back in his bunk with the door between him and the pilothouse closed. Part of the floor had to be picked up so Ralph could get to the gas tank and pump. There were nets and other things stored under the floor, as well. They were helping him when a big wave hit the *Randelyn*, throwing Ralph off balance. His head hit a shelf and the can of gas went into the heater and the storage area below. There was an explosion, which blew off one of the doors and all the windows. Ralph was a ball of fire from top to bottom. He jumped out the open door into the ocean, never to be seen again. All of Frank's back was on fire, but he was still functioning. He slowed down the engine and kicked open the door to where Byron was sleeping, then he went out of the other pilot house door to jump into the ocean. He hit a big chain that was part of the rigging ran down the side of the boat and it threw him back on deck. In an instant, the water on the deck rolling back and forth with the boat put the fire on him out. Kenneth got some gas on one foot. When he hit the deck, the water put it out, but he was hysterical, and of no help.

Byron got the two fire extinguishers and set them off in the pilothouse. He told Kenneth to go to the engine room and get them out of it; he had to slap him hard to get him to move. Even with his burns, Frank got up and helped him. Byron got the deck hose and turned it on the pilothouse; the boat was going around in circles.

They fought that fire for more than two hours before it looked like they were getting it under control. With the fire extinguishers and the water, they finally got it out. Now it was time to think about getting ashore. All the equipment and wiring was burned out of the pilothouse; the compass was broken; not a light would burn. All they had going for them was

Cecil Swindell aboard the Randelyn at Bayou La Batre, AL., 1956

that the engine was still running and they knew about where they were by the running time from the Beaufort-Morehead inlet.

Byron asked Frank if he thought the wind had changed. Frank told him he didn't think it had, so figuring the wind was still coming from the northwest, he put it on the starboard bow and headed for shore. It was about eleven o'clock and total darkness; the only thing he had to steer by was the way the waves were hitting the bow.

He stayed at the wheel for twenty-four hours. The spray from the water and the wind coming in through the windows made the temperature about forty degrees. Frank said he was sure Byron had a lot on his mind at that time; he had no idea where they would hit the beach.

Frank Leary

Frank took off what was left of his old clothes, put on some more good warm clothes, and got in his bunk. Kenneth was looking after his foot and was lying down, still not mentally right. As they were heading in, the muscles in Frank's legs were tightening and pulling his legs up under him; he was in a lot of pain. Byron told him that wherever they hit the beach, he was going to run the boat ashore and try to get some help to get them to a hospital.

At about ten o'clock the next night, Byron saw something on the beach. He told Frank he thought it was the water tank at Charleston, South Carolina, and it was. As they were heading into the inlet, they came up to another boat. Byron stopped them and told them to radio the Coast Guard and have some medical personnel and ambulances there; he told them what time they would be there. Frank said they were waiting for them when they got there. They lifted him off, sheet and all. His heels were against his back. They were in the hospital for about seven weeks before they got to come home.

Frank still has the scars of this accident. He said he told Byron the last time he saw him that he owed his life to him; he said that if Bryon hadn't taken control like he did, with good sane thinking, they would not have made it. Byron told him that if he had shut down the engine, it would have been the end because the water from the deckhouse was what had made the difference.

The *Randelyn* was fixed up again, but Byron gave it up a few years later. It stayed in Florida where other people worked it. I don't think it ever was a big money maker for anybody. In the Mariel boatlift from Cuba, it was run over there to bring people back to the U.S. It hit something on the bottom as they were tying up over there in the harbor in Cuba, and sank. The crew got off and got on another boat; it was left there.

Knowing about some of the life of this boat, if that woman said she had put a curse on it, it looked like it might have come true. There are some who believe it did.

(This accident happened in December 1956 or 1957.)

Sailboats

While waiting for the drawbridge to close recently, I noticed that the sailboats going through it today are very different from what they were years ago. Today's sailboats have a steel mast, nylon sails, and are made of fiberglass, with nice colors to make them pretty. I have some fond memories of the old sailboats and a lot of stories my father told me about the life and crews that were on them. There are some men still with us who used to sail them, but all that's left of the boats are pictures.

I told one story about taking them to the railways to have the bottoms repaired and painted, but much more than that had to be done in order to keep them working; some of it I would call major work.

In the late summer, for instance, I can remember seeing the sails of these boats spread out in different people's yards, and men sitting around them in chairs with part of the sail pulled up into their lap, sewing up seams and patching holes. They used a crooked needle when it was needed, and a piece of leather on their hand to push it. It was called a "palm". Right at the base of the thumb was a little round piece of metal that looked like a rivet that had a small place in the center that just fit the end of the needle. The needle went through and back out on the topside. They used beeswax on the string they were using - it made it work better and also helped preserve it.

Some of these men were old and not physi-  cally able to go to sea anymore, but they knew how to fix a sail. I'm sure they felt useful and were helping out where they could. These sails were made of canvas and were very heavy. Mr. Sam Williamson did a lot of this type of work for different people.

Mr. Sam Williamson

In getting the boats ready to go to work, another important thing that was checked was the mast. A man was hoisted to the top of it in a bosun chair, from which he scraped all the old varnish off and checked the mast for rotten wood all the way down to the deck. If nothing wrong was found with it, it was repainted with varnish, usually a couple of coats. It had to be slick in order for the hoops attached to the sails to go up and down with no problem.

The mast was replaced when rotten wood was found; usually it was where the mast went through the deck. If the mast broke out with the sails up, the crew had a real problem getting the sails and rigging aboard. Then they had to be towed in; there was no way they could move without the sails. It did happen, occasionally.

There was a storm one year; just about all the masts were broken out of those Sharpies around Core Sound. The men from that area had to go up Neuse River to find trees suitable to make new masts out of. In every community, there was a man they called on to go into the woods and pick out the tree to be used; generally, he was a carpenter. There were some who could just look at the bark and tell whether it would make a good mast or not. (My brother says he still can.) The size and length of the tree was important; one was chosen so that the least amount of work was needed to make it a mast.

When the tree was finally cut down, the first thing they did was measure off and cut it to the length the mast was going to be. The next thing was take the bark off. (I'm told these old yard spades did a good job, as well as drawing knifes and saws.) It was then measured and marked with a chalk line from one end to the other, then they went to work with an ax and another type of wood tool called an "adze" to chop it out and make it square. It was now considered that the most work was done.

They would then get about a dozen men together to go into the woods with cross sticks to put under the tree and bring it out and get it close to the boat they were going to put it on. They would prop it on its edge and go to work on it again, chopping off the corners to make it octagonal. (8 corners, then to 16, to 32.) Where it went through the deck, it was left octagonal so that wedges could be used to tighten it. From the deck up, they went to work with wood planes to make it round and smooth; it was also varnished.

If there were no boats around to use to "step it" as it was called, three smaller poles were tied together and stood on end in a tripod over the hole so it could be hoisted into place.

I saw Mr. John Hopkins make a mast up on the side of the Intracostal Waterway for one of his boats, one time. I don't know where he got the tree, or how long he had worked on it, but it was pretty when he got done with it. If a mast was needed in a hurry, five or six men were hired; they could make one in a day.

179

The bigger the boat, the bigger the mast. Sometimes, if a mast taken out of a bigger boat was rotten at the deck, it could be cut off and used in a smaller boat. George Clark at Belhaven had taken the mast out of one of his bigger boats; my daddy and Uncle Fred heard about it and found out it would be long enough for the *Virgil* after it was cut off. We took one of the boats we used for haul netting and went to Belhaven. They rolled the old mast overboard and we towed it home and used it.

Going and getting that mast was when I got my first taste of so-called ice cream; you couldn't buy it here. We went up to a little store at the head of the dock and the lady told us she didn't have real ice cream, she had some imitation ice cream. We all got us a cone full. It was frozen milk with chopped-up orange and lemon peels in it and some cherries to make it pretty. Somehow, my first bite got hooked in my teeth and I pulled it out of the cone. It rolled down my arm to my elbow and onto the ground and I lost it. Daddy got me another one. It was not one of the best-tasting things I had ever tasted, but it was during the War and that was all there was; it could sure have used some improvement.

The Sounding Pole

A few days ago, I was on one of the modern trawlers that ties up at the R. E. Mayo Fish Company dock, and I was amazed at all the electronic equipment that was in the pilot house. I saw radar (this tells the Captain what is going on around him), a loran and plotter (this tells the Captain

My sketch of a sounding pole

where he is), two fathometers to tell him how deep it is, two compasses - one for the automatic pilot and one for the Captain when he is steering - and a lot of radios of all kinds.

When I went to work with my daddy in the early 40's, there was very little equipment of any kind onboard. Daddy had a compass, but it was under the bow, stowed away. I seldom saw him take it out. I never saw a compass on any of the other boats that I went on, either. If they had one, it was stowed away, too. But those fishermen had their way of knowing where they were at all times and how deep the water was so they knew which way to steer their boats to get where they wanted to go. What they used was called a "sounding pole". This served as a loran, a plotter, and a compass, and was used just as much in the winter for oystering as it was in the summer for fishing; it was used year-round.

Because of it, they knew the bottom of Pamlico Sound like you know the palm of your hand.

Great care was taken in the selection of the trees to be used to make this sounding pole; they were almost always made from pine saplings. They would look for new growth pines that were growing real thick together. One sapling would always try to outgrow the other; so they were all tall and slender with only few limbs on them, and what there was, only at the very top. Each one needed to be at least fifteen feet long, with very little difference in diameter from the top to the bottom.

After they had cut the trees and taken them out of the woods, they would skin all the bark off. (Where there had been a limb, that little bulge would be cut off to make it as smooth as possible.) Then they would go to the big end and cut it at an angle, making it have a flat side of at least twelve inches. They then took a hand plane and made it as smooth as possible. This was done to both poles. They were then put together and nailed and smoothed off where the joint was. This made the pole twenty- four to twenty-eight feet long. It was then laid down, as straight as possible, to let it dry out until it was ready to use.

181

When they were putting supplies aboard the boats or getting ready to go fishing or oystering, they would put that sounding pole aboard very carefully and place it in a rack that was designed to hold it. Usually, when we were going from harbor to harbor during the day after the work was done, and getting ready for the next day, the sounding pole wasn't needed; but if they were going to put the nets back out, the bottom was sounded-out, so they could put the nets where the bottom felt right. In the wintertime during oyster season, all the oyster lumps in the deepest channels of Pamlico Sound were sounded-out, and buoys put on their edges, so they would know how to work them before the dredges were ever put in the water. (Most oystermen think the steamboats throwing their coal cinders overboard started these lumps; I have caught some myself on these lumps).

Not everybody could use that sounding pole - it had to go in the water just right. If it got caught wrong when it went into the water, it could knock somebody overboard, it would break, or it would pull the man using it overboard if he didn't turn it loose. Usually, it was the Captain or a man who knew how to use it and could tell the Captain what the bottom felt like in a language they both understood. You could hear words like muddy, oozy, soft, shelly, hard, crusty, muddy on top, hard underneath, it's dropping off, it's coming up, we are on the edge, we are in the mud, etc. If the Captain was sounding and somebody else was steering and he said, "Let her go," that meant to hold present course. If it was calm and he said, "Hold her off a little," that meant to change course a few degrees toward the deeper water. If he said, "Hold her in," you turned toward the shallow water a few degrees.   You had a different set of rules if the wind was blowing. If it was blowing against the boat on the side you were standing on and you heard, "Hold her up a little," that meant to turn toward the wind a few degrees. If you heard, "Let her fall off a little," that meant to let the wind blow the boat around a few degrees. This didn't have anything to do with the water depth - it could have been deeper or shallower. The Captain knew in his mind the kind of bottom he was looking for and he knew about how to steer the boat to find it. I would say that ninety-eight percent of the time, these soundings were made in total darkness, usually from two to four in the morning.

When we worked out of Brant Island, these men knew that the calm hours were from about midnight to two o'clock in the afternoon. With their boats being small and the net skiffs even smaller, in order to go into Pamlico Sound, this was the time slot they had to work in. Anytime after midnight that the first engine was started, you knew the race was on; sometimes you didn't take time to put your clothes on until after the anchor was pulled and you were underway. Some hauls, as they were called, were better than others, and everybody had in their mind which one they wanted. There is on each side of Brant Island Shoal, an area on the bottom, of ocean-size clamshells and most of the time this was considered to be the best haul, but it was also about the furthest out these men wanted to go.

When we got clear of Brant Island and got to about twelve feet of water, you could see arrangements being made to go to using the sounding pole; you would see a man go to the stern and take it out of the rack and over hand it until he was holding it at the center. When he got ready, you would see the leading end go into the water. The boat was now traveling at about four miles an hour and the pole had to go down exactly parallel with it. As it was going down, he would overhand it toward the top until it hit the bottom. Usually it was straight down by this time. Sometimes he would jump it up and down two or three times to get a better feel of the bottom; then he would pull it back up a few inches and let the force of the water carry it on back until it became level. Now the other end was leading and ready to go down unless he decided to hold it before letting it go again; it was a smooth operation.

When I think back, I can see how remarkable their knowledge of Pamlico Sound was. When we headed offshore in the wee hours of the morning, each crew was dragging almost a mile of nets and had a small light burning in the cabin. You could only see if you were looking in the back door or through a crack in the cabin. Using that sounding pole to steer by, at sunrise you could see how accurate they were in not over-lapping one another's rig, and each crew would get done at about the same time.

One last thing: the art of making a good sounding pole has not left us yet! I have talked to several people on the island and the surrounding areas and there are still some men here that can make a first-class sounding pole, if anybody should ever need one.

Working at the Fish House

I see a lot of our young people today walking along the road, and most of them will tell you there is nothing much to do around here. There may be a lot of truth in what they say, but I can tell you it wasn't that way when I was growing up here. There was plenty to do! A lot of times, I didn't want to do it. Sometimes, Mama had to use a little "per-suasion" to get me moving.

We had chickens, hogs, a cow, and a mule called Old Bill. All the ani-mals had to be fed; the cow had to be milked twice a day. I guess by the time I didn't need a diaper anymore, I was feeding-up and gathering the eggs while Mama milked the cow.

We would shuck corn and take an old hand corn sheller and shell the corn off the cob until we had enough for the next feeding. Then, off to the barn loft to get hay for the cow and Old Bill to eat during the day . . . this was the good part.

You could see for miles around. All the land that could be farmed was farmed, and I can tell you, this was the part I didn't like. I know how to chop corn and cotton using a hoe, doing a row at a time. I was never

184

known to be a first-class cotton picker; everybody else could pick two hundred pounds a day. I was lucky if I got twenty-five pounds. I also knew how to gather corn using an old mule and cart. I knew at an early age that I didn't want any part of farming, but I loved to fish.

I know now that living here, we didn't know much about the outside world, back then. If we visited other people who lived fairly close, we walked; we would hook up Old Bill to the cart to go longer distances. If we were going to other communities, we would walk to the boat landing and use the boat. World War II was going on and all the young men had been drafted, leaving only the old men and us schoolboys here. The farmers were really in need of help and they needed help at the fish houses at the bridge here, too. This is where a bunch of us boys went.

Otis Gibbs

This was a new experience for all of us. There were a bunch of black men working there; I mean some big men, including Clyde Smith his brother Dallas. They were handling three hundred pound blocks of ice like most people handle a loaf of bread. Others included: Otis Gibbs, Major and Jimmie Jarvis, John Johnson, Willie Jennette,

John Johnson

James Jones, and others who have slipped my mind, except for Louis Credle, the "Mouth of the South." I'm sure he could out talk Eddie Murphy, anytime. He never met a stranger and you could always tell where he was working, because you could hear him. They were all hard-working men who did everything from icing the boats to loading the trucks, stacking those one hundred and twenty-pound boxes of fish six-high in those trucks

I, along with the other boys, was not sure this was the place to be, but Captain Ralph Mayo and Captain Roland Styron told us they had a job for us, so we went to work. They had me dragging fish from the people who were culling them to the man who was weighing, icing, and packing them into the boxes - about sixty pounds at a time. This beat cotton picking, and the money wasn't bad, either!

Fred Mason

Some days, when a lot of fish were caught, we would work into the night. As we worked and learned, we got to do different jobs, so I think we fitted in pretty well. It was a fairly big work force. As we worked, the fish dealers would stand around waiting to get their trucks loaded. There was money in every pocket, and I mean rolls of money. After a while, we would see them arranging fish boxes in a circle with one on its side. We knew there was going to be a poker game getting underway. Everybody who wasn't working would be watching the game or playing, if they could afford it. They played for big money, too. On days when there were delays in the run boats coming in with the fish, there would be two games going on: the fish dealers would have their own game, betting anywhere from one to five dollars, and our game, where we would be betting one to five cents. Sometimes, it took us longer to play a hand

James Hopkins

than it took the others; it could take a while for Major or Otis to make up their minds to raise the bet to two cents or not.

If the fish dealers dropped a coin on the dock and it went through the cracks, it broke our game up. If it was a quarter or a fifty-cent piece, we looked like wharf rats going over the side and underneath the dock to plow around in the mud, water, and fish scales, looking for the money!

Sometimes we found it, and sometimes we didn't, but you can believe we were all wet and muddy and didn't smell too good, either. Then it was time to go swimming -clothes and all - and swim until the boat came in.

One day I went into the water so fast, I forgot to give somebody my wallet to hold, and lost it. Somewhere, there is a wallet in the water around here with two crisp "Silver Certificate" one-dollar bills inside it. I'm not going to tell you where I lost it, because somebody just may go looking for it. I plan to go looking myself when I get time. Who knows? I just may find it (but the dollar bills won't be so crisp any more).

I enjoyed working in the fish house. I met lots of folks and we have remained good friends throughout the years. It is one of the times in my life I don't want to forget.

P.S. Clyde is the father of Bubba Smith, the football player. John Johnson was about the last man to work there, of this crew.

Stories Daddy Told Me

Daddy told us about his first job on an old sail boat. It was operated by Mr. Billy Howard Lupton and Daddy was the cook. I don't guess that procedure has changed over the years: I think even now, the first job you get on these big boats is to be cook.

Mr. Billy had a dog on the boat with them that ate the scraps that were left over from the meals. Daddy said one night he had fixed supper and put down what was left for the dog to eat. When he went out to get some water from overboard and started to washing the dishes, he looked over. The plate the dog was eating on was empty. He had licked it completely clean, so Daddy said he picked it up and threw it right into the plate locker.

My daddy told me this: It used to be that when oysters were caught on those old sailboats and got them loaded, you raced to get to the docks ahead of everybody, either at Washington or New Bern. The first boat in got the best place to sell at the head of the dock.

One time, there was a man named Mr. Charlie Sadler on one of those sailboats. When they sold all their oysters and Charlie got his money, he went up the street in Washington. When he came back, he had bought himself a brand new suit; everything including socks, shoes, tie, and hat - all of it for eight dollars.

There wasn't a small pocket where we normally put our handkerchief at the upper left lapel, so one of the men on the crew asked him why there was no pocket up there. Charlie told them that they had run out of the first-class material the suit was made out of and they didn't want to put anything shoddy on it.

Walter's Brant Island Story

Since I have been writing these stories about our past, it has been especially rewarding to me to be able to sit down with these older folks and listen to them talk about their lives and what was going on around them. There's a story about some men who were on Brant Island when the 1913 storm hit. I have known many bits and pieces about it just about all of my life, but not enough to put it together.

Then a few weeks ago, I was in the company of a fellow I used to work with. He told me of this ninety-one year old gentleman from Hobucken who got married and moved to Campbell's Creek years ago. He said I should go and talk to him - he had some interesting stories to tell. He said his name was Mr. Walter Sadler.

I went over a few weeks ago and met him. I used to know his mother and daddy when I was a boy. We talked about a lot of things and the subject came up about the men on Brant Island. He knew a lot of the details of what went on because his daddy was one of the men. Here it is.

There were six men on the island; four of them were Gaskills from Cedar Island, one was Mr. Ira Carawan, who was living at that time at Hog Island and moved later to Hobucken, and the other was Mr. Johnnie Sadler from Hobucken. There were two men to a crew, so they had three skiffs for fishing the nets, and three camps for the crews to stay in.

When they got up on the morning of September 2nd, it was blowing too hard for them to fish their nets. As the day went on, the weather got worse; it was blowing and raining harder, so they had to keep their boats bailed out and put out more lines to hold them. The water was coming up over the island, so they had to do something with the nets they had spread out on the marsh. There was a small sailboat mast by one of the camps, which they tied to the camps to keep from floating away.

Some time during the evening, Walter says something happened with the weather. The water started rising so fast, it made these men change the way they were thinking. They realized that the things they were trying to hold onto were no longer important. They knew it was time to think about surviving.

Mr. Sadler said they made a very quick and important decision: they got the sailboat mast and loaded it into the biggest skiff and all six men got in. He don't know whether the water was deep enough for the skiff to float over the island, or if they should go up the cove close to the camps to the center of the island in back of the tall reed-like grass, and put out the best anchor they had.

As soon as it is set, a boat anchored like this swings back and forth. They saw they didn't need this skiff to do that; it needed to head directly into the wind at all times. At about the center of the swing, they got the sailboat mast, took it to the bow, stood it on its end, and turned it loose. Walter said his daddy didn't know just how far down in the mud it went, but with the weight of it, it went down a long way. They then put the bow-line to it, so it would hold them in place.

It was before sundown and this was all they had to work with. Now there was nothing else to do but keep the water bailed out of the skiff and pray they would make it. I'm sure it was the longest night they ever lived. According to what other people have told me about this storm, the wind and water continued to rise all night. It was a very dark night and these men had no way of making a light. Walter says his daddy told him the water was very rough all around them, but that it was a little smoother where they were.

When daylight came, the water was still rising; it got to where they could barely see the tops of the tall reed-like grass. It was still blowing more a hundred miles an hour and raining very hard in the squalls. When the eye passed over at about ten o'clock, the rain and wind let up enough so they could see. Everything on the island was gone; there was no sign of their other skiffs or nets, and no sign of the camps they had stayed in.

After the eye passed, the wind changed direction and the water started to go out. It was still blowing hard, but they knew the weather conditions were going to improve.

The men were concerned about how the folks at home had made out. They knew, too, that their families would be wondering about what had happen to them.

Sometime before sundown, the wind dropped down enough so that they decided to try to make it up Middle Bay (the closest landing to them) so everybody would know they were all right. When they opened the engine house that covered that old nine-horse Bridgeport engine, they had no idea whether it would run or not. A lot of water - both fresh and salt - had blown around it.

Walter says his daddy got it primed and ready to run. When he pulled the crank up on the flywheel the first time, it grabbed and started to run. His daddy said that he had heard talk of sweet music before, but that this was the sweetest music he ever heard in his lifetime.

They went up the main shoal to Terrapin Island before turning over towards Middle Bay. They got up Middle Bay okay. The water was waist deep on the end of the road, but they got out and tied up the skiff and walked home before sundown. Mr. Sadler's family was mighty glad to see him walking in; they had made out all right upstairs at the home. The old hat he was wearing had no brim anywhere around it; it had been blown off. He was wearing just the crown.

A little bit of history on Walter: he was born at Hobucken in 1906, across the road from the Barnett Cemetery. He graduated from Hobucken School in 1925 and went to Atlantic Christian College in 1926. He moved to the University of North Carolina in 1927 and went there for almost two years.

He realized he was putting a lot of stress on his family with the other things in the family going on, so he quit and came home to work.

A short time later, he married Myra Mayo from Campbell's Creek and built a home alongside his daddy, here in Hobucken.

With Myra's getting the family home place at Campbell's Creek, they sold out and moved there in 1936, where they remained and raised their family and he farmed.

Walter says it took all day to move over to Campbell's Creek; the road was impassable in January. There was no road other than a cart path from Silver Hill to Small; he had two old trucks loaded up. They had to go to Bridgeton, over to Chocowinity and back down to Campbell's Creek.

Myra passed away in 1970; Walter has been alone since then. He's in good health for a man ninety-four years old. His yard is full of flowers and he keeps a good size garden.

This is a good story, I'm glad to have gotten it before it left us.

Years ago, there was an old man who lived here. People didn't know much about him or his family, if he had any. The only thing they knew for sure was that he was bad to get along with; a lot of people were scared of him. Nobody had anything good to say about him; he seemed to be a bad person - that was the opinion of everybody.

When he passed away, somebody from Vandemere came and took his body back for burial. Some people from here went, just to see what a preacher could say about this person.

When they body was set be buried a Preacher moved over, stood for a few seconds, and said: "We have come together to bury this man. I'm not going to have much to say about him. We are going to bury him and let whoever claims him, come and get him. We are dismissed."

Building the Intracoastal Waterway

Many years ago, when almost all shipping was done by water, most of the time it was the weather that determined whether a ship could sail or not. Many men and ships were lost at sea because of the storms and rough seas that sailed up and down our coast in the ocean.

The Intracoastal Waterway from New High Rise Bridge

The leaders of our country saw that there needed to be waterway that connected the inland waters up and down our coast so that the weather would not have to be considered and the trading of commerce could be done in protected waters on a dependable schedule. This was most vital for the survival of our country.

In 1918, the first surveyors came here to lay out where the inland waterway was to be cut. Several men from here were hired; Rufus Mason, Charlie Jones, and Sam Swindell were three of them. The route they finally chose started at the mouth of Goose Creek at the side of Pamlico River, going up the creek to almost the head and cutting through to the head of Jones Bay, and from this on through to Gales Creek, then running down it to Bay River.

With today's regulations, I doubt this waterway would have been cut where it is, because of the impact it had on this area. (Not only that, but the head of Goose Creek was full of alligators. It was an ideal place for them - it was fresh water and had very little movement unless it rained.) A place called Sal's Orchard was directly in the path where the waterway was going to be cut. Charlie Jones, who was born and raised in that area, told me he didn't know how it got its name. It was about an acre in size, with a little hill on it, and was full of mercule bushes, the ideal nesting place for alligators. They were all over the area and could be seen at the bridge at times. Charlie said that one time, Mr. Joe Balance came up from Sal's Orchard with a bucketful of alligator eggs he was taking to the commissary; Charlie said they looked mighty big to him.

In 1928, a thirty-inch dredge named the *Currituck* came and started cutting the waterway at the mouth of Goose Creek, deepening and widening it as they went. When they got to Sal's Orchard, there were big and small alligators all over the place, as well as some coming out of the pipeline.

Sam Swindell said he saw some little alligators in one of those old kitchen-type match boxes on one of the service boats, and Charlie said

193

Tommy Leary came out of there with one in a gunshot box. My brother, Thomas, saw a big one on top of a little boat; it had been cut into by the cutter head of the dredge and they had a sawed-off stick jammed into its mouth to hold it wide open. Occasionally, you hear about somebody seeing an alligator in different areas today, but I haven't heard of anybody seeing any where Sal's Orchard used to be in my lifetime.

The word had been put out that they were going to cut the road into the waterway at about nine o'clock one night. A lot of people gathered to watch it but the dredge broke down. (They had all gone home by the time they finally crossed it.) They had everything in place for the people to get across. As soon as the pipeline was out of the way, they put a cable across the cut, tightened it up, and put a barge with a man on it to pull it back and forth as needed. He had some hooks with handles to catch on the cable. They started building the old swing bridge right away and a lot of people from here were hired to help.

When they got to Jones's Bay, the dredge had a problem with big cypress stumps jamming the pump. The old folks didn't know about them because they were under water and had been hacked off. I heard my father speak about them, as well as others; they wondered who had cut them off like that. (I know how the Indians built their canoes; I think they probably cut them off and made canoes out of them many years ago.)

A lot of people - both black and white - lived around Spring Creek. A big logging operation was going on and Kernel Jacobs had broken a lot of land out in that area for farming. The tracks were laid out from the south side of Spring Creek and went almost to the southeast side of the island, with other tracks branching off in different directions. All the logs were brought here by a steam engine, rolled overboard, and then put on a raft to be towed to Washington by tugboat. There was a doctor who lived in the Spring Creek community, as well as a school for black children and a church just over the bridge on the left. The commissary was the company store.

Another downside of cutting this waterway where they did is that it put salt water where fresh water used to be. You would think that cutting it from one creek to another would not make much difference, but it did. With the layout of the shoals in Pamlico Sound being where they are, the waterway serves as an equalizer between Pamlico River and Neuse and Bay Rivers and Jones Bay. Water is flowing through it one way or another all the time; in hurricanes and other types of severe weather, it sometimes flows as fast as five to seven miles an hour. The shoals I'm writing about stretch from the east side of the island to where Brant Island was and on into the Pamlico Sound for another five miles toward Ocrakoke. These shoals have no more than a foot of water going over them in places; altogether, it's about eight miles from this island. In a northeaster, the water comes down the sound in the deep water and goes around the end of it, heading up Neuse and Bay Rivers and Jones Bay. It is somewhat trapped; the only way to relieve it is through the waterway.

A lot of the land that was being farmed on the west side of this island had to be given up when they cut it. The land had flooded before, but it was fresh water. When it flooded after the waterway was cut, the water was salt. Michael Lewis of Lowland said that his folks lived and farmed some of the land between Spring Creek and Lowland. He told me that the water came up and killed the fruit trees and fig bushes in their yard, and all the grass that the animals were fed on. They had to give the land up at a time when a family needed land in order to grow crops to survive. Had it not been for this waterway, many men and ships would have been torpedoed by the submarines operating just off our coast during World War II. A lot of war goods were moved up and down our coast - and lives were saved - during that period through this waterway.

My Dad's Experience in the 1913 Storm

At this time of the year, we usually hear a lot about hurricanes; about the destruction they bring and how people live through them. I think, by far, the worst one that ever hit this area was on September 2, 1913. I would like to share with you what was going on with two people I know. One was my father, Mr. Charlie Spain, and the other was Mr. Emory Sadler.

My father and Mr. Joe Sadler (no relation) owned a two-masted sail boat about fifty feet long known as a "Sharpie." At the time of this hurricane, Daddy and Mr. Emory were hauling fish from the fish house on Sow Point to Washington, North Carolina, making a trip every other day. On September 2nd, they were on their way back to Sow Point. The further they got down the Pamlico River, the more wind and squalls there were, with high wind and rain. By the time they got to Bath Creek, every time a squall hit they would have to drop their sails and anchor until the winds and rain passed; then they would pick it up and go on. Between each squall, the wind would increase a little.

When they got down to Indian Island, the wind was constant at fifty to sixty knots and it was close to sundown. They decided to go to the back of Indian Island and anchor. My father told me there was really no smooth side it was blowing so hard. They anchored - putting out both anchors - just before good dark. They weren't far from shore on the inward swing when the anchors became set.

The wind and rain continued to increase and one of the cables to the anchors stranded just after dark. My father said he told Mr. Emory that if the winds continued to increase the cables weren't going to hold, but they made no plans as to what they were going to do if it happened.

Sometime before midnight, it got to raining so hard that they couldn't see Indian Island on the inward swing and were waiting for something to happen. Finally, an hour or so before daylight, they broke loose. As luck would have it, the boat turned completely around and got the stern up in the wind; when it started ahead, it gave them some control of the boat.

They hadn't gone far when the yaw boat lying across the hatches was picked up by the wind and stood up on its bow end against the mast and rigging. This acted as a sail. They got to going so fast that Daddy said he got a funny feeling in his stomach and knew they had to get it down. In the process of getting it down, they lost control of the boat and came side to. They thought the boat would roll over when this happened, but it didn't. They drifted for a short time and finally went into some small oak trees. Mr. Emory jumped off into three feet of water. Daddy realized they were going to become separated, so he ran forward and jumped off and let the boat go. They were holding onto the trees as the waves washed right over them; he got to thinking that it looked like the end was near.

They started to move from tree to tree between the waves until Mr. Emory got to a tree and felt with his feet that a fence was nailed to it. They decided to follow it. It led them out to a house at Hickory Point that had a skiff tied to the front porch. They were still in about two feet of water. Thinking that the house was empty, they got behind it to get out of the wind and rain. After about two hours, they heard some noises inside and realized there was somebody in there.

A man named Mr. Jim Kurman came to the door and invited them in. The water continued to rise until it came into the house, so they moved upstairs and weathered out the rest of the storm. When it was over, they helped Mr. Jim take his skiff back to the creek and he took them across South Creek. They walked down to Goose Creek and got across to Lowland and walked to Hobucken.

There had been about eight feet of water here, and my mother and oldest sister had weathered out the storm upstairs at Uncle Jack's place, and were all right. Daddy and Mr. Emory stayed home for about four days before going back to look for the boat. They went up South Creek for almost five miles before they found it up in the trees on the west side, about a half mile from the water. The bottom was probably seven feet off

197

the ground. Daddy said you could walk under it without bending over and had to reach up to touch the bottom.

I think we have had some pretty bad storms in my lifetime, but I don't believe we ever had one as bad as this one was in 1913.

The 1913 Storm

Since I wrote about Uncle Jack in the last story about the 1913 storm, I thought it would be a good time to talk about what else was going on in Hobucken at that time. This information was told to me by Rufus and Lillian Mason, who live right here by me. They were both there in the storm with their families; they were both eight-years old. My mother and my oldest sister were there, too. The story I wrote about my father's experience during the storm was in The Pamlico News in 1985.

Mr. Rufus's family lived in a single-story house where the pavement ends here on the main road in Hobucken. Mr. Dick Parson lived a little farther down. (Mr. Wash Ireland lived down there, too.) On the morning of September 2, Mr. Rufus said the water was coming up from Drum Creek right up the main road in the community and it was rising fast

Mr. Wash Ireland had a kunner tied up at Drum Creek. (A kunner was a big canoe with one end squared.) The kunner broke loose and the water was bringing it up towards the end of the road when Mr. Dick Parson got hold of it and tied it to his front porch post.

As the water continued to rise and the wind and rain got worse, that kunner broke loose and started up the road again. Mr. Rufus said that his daddy saw it coming and went out and got a line on it and tied it to their house. There was about a foot of water in the house by this time.

In back of their house was a smaller house where they kept fire wood and some shelves to put other things on. Mr. Rufus said that at the time

Uncle Jack Lupton's House 1920.

of the storm, the firewood was stacked all the way to the top. His daddy was out there picking up everything and putting it up in the rafters. He had a gallon of kerosene which he tied to the rafters, too. Mr. Rufus's mother was inside putting up everything she could. There were about fifty or sixty chickens in the yard, but there was nothing anyone could do about them; they had to look out for themselves.

Later on in the day, they decided to get in that kunner and go up to Uncle Jack's place. (He had a ten-room, two-story house he had built himself.) The water was now between two and three feet deep in Mr. Rufus's house and it was coming in fast; Mr. Rufus said that if they had stepped off the porch when they came out to leave, their hats would have floated.

When they got to Uncle Jack's place, about forty people were already there. The women and children were upstairs, and the men were downstairs. The water continued to rise all night and everybody was getting hungry. On towards daylight, Mrs. Joella Sadler and Clyde Styron, who operated the Ben Sadler store, told the men she thought there was a case of animal cookies high enough on a shelf in the store so that it would be dry, so some men took a kunner and went and got them for the children to eat.

199

Mr. Rufus said that the water had continued to rise and was now about half way up Uncle Jack's windows, with waves washing through the windows right into the house. My grandfather, W.T. Emory, came up with his family, Aunt Edith and Dea. They had gotten into his kunner through one of the upstair windows of their house.

The high point of the water, Mr. Rufus said, was about nine a.m. on Sept. 3rd when the eye of the storm passed over. By ten o'clock, the wind had changed and the water started to go out. By twelve, it had gone out two feet or more, so that towards evening, people were anxious to get back to their homes to see how much damage had been done. (My father's and mother's house had floated off the blocks and was resting against some fruit trees on the east side of their land.)

Mr. Rufus said that when they got home, everything in the house was resting upside down where it had been floating before the water left. He said he helped his mother put things back in place, and that the house itself was all right.

All the chickens had drowned and the water was all gone off the land, so his daddy got some of the dry wood out of the back house and the gallon of kerosene and started to get a fire going under the wash pot. They had some fresh water in a barrel that hadn't turned over and they came up to the Sadler store and got some flour. (Their flour had gotten wet.) When he got back home, Mr. Rufus's father started to picking up and skinning those chickens; with his mother making dumplings in the house, it wasn't long before they had a pot full of chickens and dumplings. They were all hungry and the food tasted mighty good - it was about two days since they had last eaten.

The next morning, his daddy cleaned the rest of those chickens. There was a fire going in the stove in the house so they made another big pot of chickens and dumplings and invited all the neighbors in to help eat it. Mr Rufus said he guesses he got a little selfish when he saw them filling up their plates, wondering whether they were going to leave any for him or not, but there was plenty for everbody. He said as he looks back he realizes it wasn't long before their lives were back to normal.

I am told that there was between seven and eight feet of water here in Hobucken. Based on the depth of the water that was up South Creek where daddy's sailboat was finally found in the trees, I believe that everything that wasn't at least eleven feet above sea level was under water in this area of Pamlico Sound during this storm.

The Billy Jones Story

This is a story about a man's amazing ability to survive when it seems like everything is against him.

His name was Billy Jones and he lived at Mesic. He was a big-built man, was in his twenties, and in excellent health.

In the middle forties, oystering was about the surest and best way to make money. The state had opened the laws up for any boat under thirty-two ft. to catch oysters using their own power or power winders to pull their dredges. A lot of people got in the business - boats were being built as fast as they could, all around Pamlico Sound. This was not like fishing; the oysters didn't move, they had been there growing and multiplying for centuries. Pamlico Sound was full of oysters. During the war the price went up, and it continued to go up. It was a good business to be in.

All the fish and oyster houses had boats from thirty-five to forty feet in length to haul fish in from the haul netters in the summer, and oysters in the winter. They had hatches on them that went from one side to the other and were about two feet wide and ten to twelve feet long, depending on the width of the boat. They had a little loop made of rope on each end so they could be lifted up by two men and stacked on the stern - one on the other - while the boat was being loaded.

In the summer, these boats were called "run boats" but in the winter they were called "buy boats" because when a man left the dock to buy oysters, he left with money in his pocket to buy them wherever he could and from anybody wanting to sell.

Billy Jones

When this man left the dock, he never knew when he would be back. There were many unknown factors as to when he could get enough oysters to come in with. The weather might be bad, so the oystermen couldn't work; some of the people he had bought from before might not be in the area he was and would sell to somebody else; or sometimes, he could get a load in the same day he went out because he was in the right place at the right time, and someone might sell to him who he hadn't bought from before.

When the weather was good, the oystermen worked until almost sundown and then came in to the closest harbor where the buy boats were to buy what they had caught that day. Most of the time, the men on these buy boats would head for the dock with their load in the night, so as to be ready to unload first thing the next morning, then head back out for another load when the oystermen came to harbor that night. If a buy boat didn't return to dock during the night, nobody got too concerned; it was figured he didn't buy enough oysters that day to come in with. If the weather was bad, it could be two or three days before he returned.

From September to November, there would be several different things going on in Pamlico Sound: if the fishermen had a good year, some of them would still be fishing, and shrimping would be still going on by a few boats. Oystering usually started the middle of September, so at this time of year there were a lot of men out in the Sound.

Billy Jones was buying oysters for Earl Holton of Vandemere, running a boat called the *Nettie M.* He went over to Great Island, which is in Hyde

202

County close to Swan Quarter. I don't know how many days he was out when he headed for Vandemere. It was dark, so he had to cross the Pamlico River down at the entrance.

After he had left the north shore heading across, he soon began to realize that his boat was taking on water - more than he could pump out. He knew it was going to sink, and he didn't have much time to prepare. When it sank, it went right on down until just the top of the mast was out of the water. The mast light was still burning, so it gave him some light to see what he could do. When the hatches floated up off it, he managed to get a hold of three of them and got them together. It was fairly rough, so it was a job to handle all three of them, but he managed for a while. With the mast light burning, he tried to head for the closest beacon, paddling to keep that mast light behind him. This was probably about ten o'clock that night.

After about three hours, that mast light went out and he lost one of those hatches. It was getting rougher all the time, and he had lost his sense of direction; now he was just drifting with the waves. The water wasn't too cold at this time of the year, so he was not fairing too bad - he knew someone would see him and pick him up during the day.

After he wasn't to the dock the next morning, nobody was worried about it, because it was figured he didn't buy enough oysters to come in with and would be in the next night. There were no radios or any other type of communication at that time.

Billy drifted with those hatches all day; nobody saw him and the current coming down Pamlico River was taking him farther out towards Ocracoke. He had lost some of his energy by sundown, and another hatch had got away from him. Just after sundown, Billy saw a small fleet of shrimp boats that was working out there. My brother-in law, Wilbur Watson, got close enough to him that he could read the name on his boat. Billy hollered, but with the engine running, Wilbur didn't hear him. He turned around and went back towards the fleet.

The wind and tide carried him towards the slew buoy, which is almost in the center of Pamlico Sound. When he got close to it, he turned that last hatch loose and got a hold of that beacon. This was about midnight. The beacon pilings was full of barnacles and as the waves washed him against them, they cut him and he started to bleed, making him lose his energy quicker. He needed water to drink; he was beginning to feel the effects of no water. He knew if no one found him that day, he wouldn't be able to make it another night. He felt like the end was near for him.

Jasper Volova, Sr. and Lee Morrison left Vandemere to go to Great Island where Billy had got his oysters; they had to go by this slew beacon to get there. When it came in sight, they got their gun out because they saw what they thought was a goose or duck around it and they was going to shoot it when they got close enough. It was said that they had him in the gun sight when they decided to hold up; that they needed to get a better look at what it was. When they got closer, they saw it was a man. They didn't know it was Billy; nobody knew he was missing. His face, arms, and body was swelled up so bad, he wasn't recognizable to look at. It was about all they could do to get him in their boat - he was so weak that he wasn't much help.

They turned around and headed back to Vandemere with him. When they got there, Billy was taken on to the hospital where he stayed about a week to recuperate and have his cuts bandaged up.

The boat stayed sunk about two weeks - it took that long to get the oysters out of it before they took a shrimp trawler, hooked the boat to it, and dragged it to Vandemere and put it on the railway.

Billy soon left the water business. He left the area, moving to New York where he went to work with Dixie Cup Co. It was a close call for Billy. Had he not been a man of above average in size and health, he probably wouldn't have made it.

I am told that later on he wanted to pay the men for picking him up.

The Sinking of the *Violet*

In my generation, a person growing up here on Goose Creek Island thought about doing nothing else for a living other than being a commercial fisherman. It was about the only way of life here, and all of us wanted to be one. You lived here, you fished here, and everything you wanted was here. For me, I think about Willie Nelson's song and the commercial fisherman: it's not a good life, but it's my life. Some fishermen may not agree with it.

There are times when things don't go right when you live this type of life; tragedy strikes, a boat sinks, lives are lost. I know firsthand about this kind of thing; the drowning of my son Bruce when his boat *Little Fellow* was capsized brings it home to me.

But this story is not about my son; it's about the trawler *Violet* sinking in the ocean off Kill Devil Hill in January 1963, when three young men lost their lives. I was out there that night.

Most of the boats used today are made of steel and fiberglass and they are used year-round. Years ago, all the boats were made of wood and men had to have a different type of boat to do different types of fishing. That meant that some part of the year, a boat would be tied up. When

The Violet tied up at Vandemere

that happened, the upper seams would be opened up. (They're the ones in the sides between the water line and the deck.) I have been down in the holds on some of those old sailboats when they were tied up for the summer. The boat might not be leaking a drop through the bottom, but you could look right through the sides. The first time out on a fishing boat in the early spring, one man had to stay at the pump for awhile until the seams swelled back together, or until we got back into calm water.

The *Violet* had been tied up at Vandemere for some time when Freddie Balance decided to get it ready and go fishing. He got James Brothers and Charlie Popperwill, from Lowland, to help him. Everybody had been fishing out of Organ Inlet and was having a fairly good season. The pattern of the flounder back then was that about the first of December, you started to catch them close to the beach north and south, just outside Organ Inlet. Right after Christmas, the flounder started to move offshore, heading for the edge of the continental shelf. Each trip, you had to go farther offshore to find them. To get to the edge of the shelf to go to work meant about seven hours of running time, straight offshore.

I don't know how many days we had been out. The way you work with the weather at that time of the year is between the different weather systems that are coming across the country. When one system is dying out, you usually have from one to five days before another takes over and drives you in. On the twenty-second of January, it was calm and the water was slick. It was a beautiful day, but the weather report was calling for a cold front to cross that night, which meant the weather was going to become real bad.

Some time during that day, we saw the *Violet* in the fleet of boats that was working, but nobody had talked to them on the radio. It wasn't known whether his radio was even working or not, and if he knew about the bad weather report.

Just before sundown, we were right alongside of them. Freddie called, "Charles!" (You could barely hear him.) He told us he was having all kinds of problems: the boat was leaking badly; the pumps were pumping about all they could; the engine was running hot; and the batteries were dead, so everything was running off the generator. Charles told Freddie that there was a very bad weather report and that he needed to head in as soon as he could. Freddie said he was going to head in when he got his net up. We never saw or heard from him after that.

When we got our net up just after it got dark, Charles said we were heading in. A lot of other boats headed in, also. We had been running about three hours when the wind hit from the north; it was blowing hard and quickly got rough and bad. There was a merchant ship just offshore; it was reporting a north wind at fifty knots.

Ordinarily, most boats don't try to come into Oregon Inlet during the night, but when we got there at about two a. m., Charles said he was going to try to make it. We made it on in and anchored just inside the inlet. Some more boats came in, too. We lay down for a bit, and in a little while Charles got up and saw that there were some planes flying offshore dropping flares, so he turned on the radio and we listened in on what was being said.

The radio said that engine had stopped on the *Violet*, the lights were out, and the pumps were not working. The boat *Seven Seas* from Wanchese ran by them; they were hollering for some help and wanted a tow. The crew from the *Seven Seas* unhooked one of their tow cables and gave them the end of it. Freddie and his crew hooked it up. It was so rough that they ran out most of the cable to avoid snatching so bad. The crew on the *Seven Seas* couldn't see anything behind them and went inside the cabin to get out of the weather.

They had been towing the *Violet* toward the inlet for some time when they realized they had stopped. A man went out onto the stern and saw that the cable was running almost straight down. The *Violet* had sunk and was on the bottom.

They immediately got on the radio and put the word out to the other boats that the *Violet* had sunk and to be on the lookout for the crew. Then they called the Coast Guard, and cut their cable to get loose, and started to look for them.

The Coast Guard had a plane in the area pretty quick, dropping flares. What fishing boats were out were looking, too, but it was after daylight before they found any of the crew. Charlie and James had on life jackets and were picked up; they had frozen to death. Freddie was never found.

There are many ideas about him; I imagine he was in the engine room trying to get the engine going. He knew that the only chance they had was to get it running again so that the pumps and lights would go back to work. It probably rolled over, it was so rough, and trapped him inside. Another theory was that there were only two life jackets onboard (highly unlikely), so that Freddie went overboard, he went on a mattress and when he froze, he washed off it. The truth will never be known.

Most of the time, when you are working and the boat and all its systems are in good shape, you get your nets aboard and everything stowed and tied down. Then everybody goes inside and lays down except one man, who stays up to keep watch.

There was a man on watch on the boat *Oriental* as they headed for the inlet. He said later that he believed he saw one of those men that night. When it's rough and the boat is rolling badly, the mast light gives good light on either side at times as it rolls down. But at the time he saw it, nobody knew that the *Violet* had gone down. Sometimes, there is a lot of trash floating around, such as crates of lemons and oranges, boards, and garbage, so he wasn't too concerned about anything floating in the water.

This is just one of the tragic things that happen in the life of a fisherman. He has a head tide to fight all the time in order to make a living.

James Brothers is buried in the Watson Cemetery and Charlie

Popperwill is buried in McGowan's Cemetery. The body of Freddie Balance was never found, but a memorial stone was put in the Balance-Leary Cemetery by his family. All are buried at Lowland, and all bear the same death date, January 24, 1963.

Lady Betty

Today is Valentine's Day, February 14, 1996. I have just come from the Barnett Cemetery, where Vernon Hopkins was put to rest. I have known Vernon all my life. I went to school with him and enjoyed working with him at different times in our lives.

In 1959, my brother Charles had traded boats and had an old Army T. boat called *Lady Betty*. It was 104 ft. long, twin screw, and sat on the water just like a duck; it didn't take much of a wave to make it roll. Charles said it rolled the worst of any boat he had ever had; he was right. When Charles got it ready to go out, Vernon, Jim Louder (he married one of Vernon's sisters), Nelson Lee and I went out with him. We didn't make a lot of money, but for the time, it wasn't bad. We packed out at Ballard's in Norfolk and you could tell before long that Charles didn't think much of

Lady Betty

209

that boat; everything had to be tied down in order for it not to beat you to death. It rolled badly, even when it wasn't very rough.

One trip, we had been out for four days and the weather was getting bad and the seas were getting rough. At daylight, Charles said that when we hauled the net up, we were going in to pack out. We got ready and sure enough, it was rough when we started to get the net. We got the net all the way up and dumped the bag; we didn't have many fish, but we had a load of jellyfish and squid that were washing from one side to the other as *Lady Betty* rolled. About the time Vernon unhooked the block from the bag to secure it, a freak sea hit us and really knocked us bad. Vernon didn't want to turn loose of the block, but the boat was rolling so badly, he had to make a quick decision to either let it go or go with it. (A block like that swinging loose was a dangerous thing; it could kill a man if it hit him, or knock him overboard.)

Vernon went to going back and forth with the jellyfish and squid that were going from side to side. Charles and I hung onto the side of the boat. Jim was holding on until he decided to turn loose and help Vernon. He got in that pile and started going back and forth, too. He got a hold of the corner of the hatchway and got slowed down a little. As Vernon went by, Jim tried to get a hold of him, and got Vernon going around and around as he went back and forth. Vernon finally told Jim to leave him alone; he was doing better by himself. The boat was beginning to slow down a little. I don't believe we had a box of fish in that mess, but I guess we were pretty lucky; nobody got hurt and we got into the dock okay. Today, Charles and Vernon are in a better place, and they are probably talking about fishing right now.

The *Lady Betty* is at the bottom of the ocean off Chincoteague, Virginia; it sank out from under Walter Stowe and his crew some years later.

❖ ❖ ❖

The *Virgil*

Recently, my family and I were having lunch at my brother's house. During our conversation, the talk turned to the old sailboats that were around when we were children. Mary, my brother Charles's wife, said there was a picture of the *Virgil* and other sailboats hanging on the wall. We got it down and started looking at it.

I had forgotten about this picture, but when I looked at it, I knew all about it; someone standing on Campbell's Creek Bridge in Beaufort County took it, and the year was about 1947.

I remember when they went to Core Sound and towed the *Virgil* back to the Intracoastal Waterway here at Hobucken. They went to cleaning it up and painting it, putting on new ropes to hoist up the sails, and sheathing the deck where the oysters fell out of the dredges.

When they got it ready, they decided to go down to Jones Bay to try it out, and I went along. It was the scariest thing up to that point in my life I had ever experienced. As we got on down the Bay, the wind was from the southwest - blowing about ten miles an hour (with higher gusts to twenty), broadside to us. They put up all the sails and I soon found myself

The Virgil belonged to Charlie Spain from 1945-55

heading for the high side; the *Virgil* would lean a good ways over and I was sure she was going to turn over when those gusts of wind hit. She got to going pretty fast.

We sailed down to Brant Island, and I was sure glad when they turned around to head back to the dock. There was something going on when they turned around - the sails were changing sides, and the booms were swinging across.

When we got back to dock, I told them I would chop the mast, the sails, and all the rigging down, and throw it over the side and use the yaw boat to push it wherever I wanted to go from now on.

During the summer these boats were not used, so they were put up in Campbell's Creek, where the water was fresh (That way, they had no problem with saltwater worms eating them up, or the weather affecting them, and it wasn't deep).

The closest boat to the bridge in the painting is the *Lois S.* It was owned by George Lupton of Lowland. My father worked it some before he and Uncle Fred bought the *Virgil*.

The boat in the upper left is the *Virgil*; it is a Sharpie and was a Core Sound design - completely flat on the bottom. When the rudder was put in the highest position and the centerboard all the way up, it needed six to eight inches of water to go in. It was built this way so it could be worked in Core Sound; Core Sound is shallow.

It could carry about six hundred tubs (five pecks per tub) of oysters when it was fully loaded. The decks would be awash sometimes, depending on how much wave action there was; sometimes they were washing against the hatch and cabin.

I have heard my daddy tell about one time they were loaded with all she could float with, and they were heading up Neuse River to the market. Uncle Fred and Peleg Bateman were on the boat. They got to talking about how little time they would have if something was to happen. They were using the yaw boat (as it was called) to push them. Daddy said, "We wouldn't have time to get the yaw boat untied from it, it would happen so quickly." Mr. Peleg went into the cabin and came out with the butcher knife and a file and went to sharpen it so that if they had to, they could cut the ropes.

The boat on the upper right is the *W.L. Rose*, owned by John Hopkins. I believe Alton Lupton was the last man to work it from here.

On the right is another Sharpie. I remember it, but have forgotten who owned it or the name of it. It might have been the *Lucy Mae*, owned by Grady Ireland of Lowland. It's sunk, but that won't hurt it; when they get ready to use it again, they will pump it up and take it on out, scrub the sides a little, and put it to work. Is is probably better off than the others. If you go down into the hold of the other boats, you can probably look through the sides of them.

When I look at these old sailboats, I see hard work. They weren't for pleasure; the work was very hard. About midway of the deck is where the dredges were pulled and the oysters were dumped. A man had to either bend over (the way you would have to if you were tying and untying your shoes all day), or get on his knees and cull them. If they were catching a lot, this went on all day. On top of that, they had to work the sails to adjust them according to the wind (a westerly wind always had higher gusts), and watch the booms as they swung across when they turned around to head back. Sam told me he had to help reef the sails nine times in one day (his hands would be bleeding from it), and try to have the deck clear when it came time to pull the dredges in again.

For the cook, a day started before daylight. He got up and prepared breakfast with eggs and bacon, hot coffee, and enough biscuits (made from scratch) to last all day. This all had to be done before daylight because as soon as you could see, the anchor was pulled and the day began.

At dinnertime, it was oysters and biscuits - the only choice you had was what size oysters you were going to eat, and how many. For supper, it was more oysters or biscuits, and molasses.

One year, my brother-in-law, Ellis Gaskill, was working on the *Virgil* with Daddy; he was cook. One evening at suppertime, he asked if anybody was hungry. He said that he wasn't, but that if they were, he would fix something. They said "no", and nothing was fixed. There were nine biscuits leftover from dinner and a while later, Ellis said he believed he would take those biscuits and eat a few oysters with them, rather than throw them overboard. He ate all of them. Daddy said he didn't know how many he would have eaten if he'd been hungry. Days when the weather was so bad they couldn't work, a pot of butter beans was put on.

The bunks on those old boats were always wet; they were under the deck on each side of the cabin and stern, and the decks leaked. Any water that was on deck - fresh or salt - meant water in the bunk. If it was raining when it came time to go to bed, they would put their rain suits on, sometimes even putting a pan over their head to keep the water from dripping in their face. Every man I talked to knew about wet bunks.

In the wintertime, if you move the seawater with anything, the phosphorous makes it glow; Sam Swindell told me he had seen his bunk do the same thing as he moved it to get in it.

After the boat was loaded and heading for the market, there was still plenty of work to be done, because all of the oysters had to be shoveled out. Until there was a market, which bought oysters, you sold them from the boat. Mr. Rufus Mason told me about a time when they unloaded at New Bern one night, then left the dock the next morning to come down

Neuse River. After they passed Oriental, they went to feeling the bottom with the sounding pole. They came across an oyster lump just off Gum Thicket Shoal, so they went to work. They loaded about 600 tubs that day, and were back up on the Neuse River to the dock to unload again the next morning.

When the weather was good and all the boats were loaded, they had to head in different locations in order to sell them.

Roscue Rice told me that when he was working with Mr. Corbitt Ireland, two boats of them went up Albemarle Sound: one went to Herford, the other one to Edenton to sell their catch. One year he said he worked nine weeks and got nine dollars for his work.

I went on the *Virgil* when it was under sail only one more time about a year later. It was on a Saturday morning - they had unloaded it on Friday night. It was too dark to bring it back to the Intracoastal Waterway, so we went early on a Saturday morning. They put up the sails before untying from the dock; as soon we took the ropes aboard the yaw boat, we headed out. After we got out clear of the dock, there was a good westerly wind blowing. Soon the sails began to fill, and as we got to where we headed down river, the wind was directly behind and one sail was put out on each side. In just a little ways, we began to tow the yaw boat; even though it was running, it couldn't keep up.

This was a different thing from before; it was a nice, peaceful feeling to have, knowing that you are making use of something you can't see and going on with the wind.

Arlie's Funeral

Today is May 15, 1995. We had the funeral for Arlie Ireland today, here at the Barnett Cemetery. I played my guitar for a group of people from area church choirs to sing "Sheltered in the arms of God".

On my way back to my truck, I walked by Mr. Will Mayo's headstone. I saw the date of death as June 28, 1949. I know where I was that day, and whom I was with.

Back then when somebody died, people stayed up all night with the body, usually at their home. It was called a wake. The night of June 28, it rained all night very hard. I was working with my daddy. We were hauling netting and working in the skiff with Mr. Rufus Mason.

During the day, we got word that a big storm was coming and to seek a safe harbor. We were at the mouth of Jones Bay, so Daddy and Uncle Fred decided to go up to Drum Creek for the night. We got up in Drum Creek about sundown, and anchored. It was raining lightly. We bailed all the water out of the skiffs and big boats and, probably by nine o'clock, went to bed. I slept across the back of the cabin, above the engine. Mr.

Rufus and Daddy each had a bunk that they dropped down and fastened to the side of the boat with a small piece of rope that went to the top of the cabin from each end of their bunks, about two feet off the floor. The rain was coming down faster all the time; it was a good night for sleeping.

Rufus Mason

Rhoda M. Parker

Daddy was a person who, as soon as he went to bed, you could soon hear him snoring. He went to sleep quickly. This night, we all went to sleep in a hurry. After Daddy had been to sleep for a while and he needed to move, he rolled over. His hand went down towards the floor and right into water. He said, "My God, fellahs, we are sunk," and went right under my bunk, knocking out the back screen. I usually get out of my bunk and fasten the end up that goes across the door, folding it over out of the way. Daddy didn't take time for this to be done; he went right to that old hand pump and went to pumping. After he had made two or three strokes with it, the leather cup that was fastened to the bottom end of the stick pulled right off.

He said, "We are in a mess. We can't pump this water out, and I've got to go to the other boat and get a new leather for this pump." It was raining about as hard as you usually see it.

All this happened before Mr. Rufus and I had got our bunks up, and we had to put up Daddy's, too. We really couldn't do much until we got it out of the way. Those bunks they slept in, you had to arrange everything on them in order for them to go far enough to hook them. If you didn't, it could be a job. I got out of mine and was trying to find a place high enough to get onto to put my clothes on. Mr. Rufus got out of his and was standing barefoot in the water. He started up with his bunk. The box of the washing powder we used to wash dishes had come apart, so the water was mighty sudsy. A can of oil Daddy had to go in the engine had turned over, so the suds and oil together made for a very slippery floor.

Mr. Rufus started up with his bunk, but just before he got it high enough to hook it, his feet went out from under him and he went on his knees on the floor. He got right back up and said, "A man needs a pair of baseball spikes on to stand up in here this morning." He finally got it up and Daddy got back with new leather to fix the pump. It wasn't long before we had most of the water out, but we had to stay up the rest of the night to keep the water pumped out and the skiffs bailed out. It continued to rain until after daybreak. I heard later it rained thirteen inches in that storm.

We had a bad night and not too much sleep, so we didn't put the nets out. It was Friday, so we came on home. I don't think anybody felt like messing with them.

This is from Mr. Rufus Mason--He says, "Boys are not any worse today than when I was a boy, they just have more things to do with." One Sunday evening, he and some other boys were roaming around in the Drum Creek area when they came across Mr. Wash Ireland's sail skiff turned bottom up on the side of a ditch where he had been working on it. The sails were spread out on the rushes so they could dry out. They decided he needed some help, so they turned it over, moved it away from the ditch just a little, and blocked it up. They then got the mast and put it in and fastened the rigging. They got the sails, put them on, and hoisted them all the way to the top. Then they tied it off, so there it set -

under full sail on the bank. It blew a gale that night from the southwest. Mr. Mason said he didn't think it blew the mast out, but they definitely caused Mr. Ireland some unnecessary work.